HELLO CHICAGO

Goodbye Pender Harbour

Democracy Eh!

By
MARY M. WHITE

PUBLISHING™

Note for Librarians: A cataloguing record for this book is available from Library and Archives
Canada at www.collectionscanada.ca/amicus/index-e.html
ISBN 1-4120-6773-1

*Printed in Victoria, BC, Canada. Printed on paper with minimum 30% recycled fibre. Trafford's print shop
runs on "green energy" from solar, wind and other environmentally-friendly power sources.*

TRAFFORD
PUBLISHING™
Offices in Canada, USA, Ireland and UK
This book was published *on-demand* in cooperation with Trafford Publishing. On-demand
publishing is a unique process and service of making a book available for retail sale to the
public taking advantage of on-demand manufacturing and Internet marketing. On-demand
publishing includes promotions, retail sales, manufacturing, order fulfilment, accounting and
collecting royalties on behalf of the author.

Book sales for North America and international:
Trafford Publishing, 6E–2333 Government St.,
Victoria, BC v8t 4p4 CANADA
phone 250 383 6864 (toll-free 1 888 232 4444)
fax 250 383 6804; email to orders@trafford.com
Book sales in Europe:
Trafford Publishing (uk) Limited, 9 Park End Street, 2nd Floor
Oxford, UK ox1 1hh UNITED KINGDOM
phone 44 (0)1865 722 113 (local rate 0845 230 9601)
facsimile 44 (0)1865 722 868; info.uk@trafford.com
Order online at:
trafford.com/05-1684

10 9 8 7 6 5 4 3 2 1

Hello Chicago

Goodbye Pender Harbour

By
MARY M. WHITE

This book is the continuing story of Rose,
a single professional woman,
her three children
and a nursing career.

For
my dear Mother
and for my children
David, Kathleen and Gary
and for the nurses
wherever you are.

Man for the field and woman for the hearth:
Man for the sword and the needle she:
Man with the head and woman with the heart:
Man to command and woman to obey:
All else confusion.

Alfred, Lord Tennyson

Preface

❦

"WHILE HER HUSBAND REMAINED ON military duty in England, Rose returned to her mother's house in Pincher Creek to await the arrival of their first born."

For several weeks Rose tried to settle down to normal living after her years in the army. It was pleasant to help around the house, to become reacquainted with her family and the townspeople.

In June she left for Calgary to stay with her friend from the farm, Myrtle Lowery. She wanted to be near her obstetrician, Dr. Fisher. David Andrew was born July seventeenth in her training school, the Holy Cross Hospital.

When David was four months old his father returned from overseas. He remained in the army and was posted to Wainwright, Alberta.

Here married life really began. It was a happy time. The family were able to rent a fully furnished, two bedroom suite on the main floor of an older home. The baby was healthy and slept the night through. The young couple soon made friends. Rose's fantasies of being cared for, of being a real woman, of staying home and enjoying a full married life, were coming true.

But her husband had difficulty giving up his army life, the only life he had known since he was nineteen. He had gone overseas in 1939, been told what to wear, where to sleep, what to eat and what to do each day. After seven years of active war service, mostly as a tank driver, he was ill equipped for civilian life.

The stresses on the marriage became enormous. A daughter, Kathleen, was born two years after David. The children were a source of great joy, but the unreal expectations of both adults continued. Often there was not enough money, and Rose's husband's drinking and gambling habits picked up in the army took their toll. Two years after the birth of Kathleen another son, Gary, was born.

Sad to say, the marriage continued to disintegrate, as many wartime marriages did. At the end of ten years Rose found herself a single parent without financial support from her husband who was unable to give anything to his family.

Rose had to rebuild her life, as she often thought, "She finally had to grow up, to shed her illusions and to go to work." There was no such thing as welfare offered to her. She returned to her profession, nursing. Rose was very fortunate to be accepted into the Calgary General Hospital which had an excellent, up to date, nursing program.

At the time of this book, Rose is the matron of St. Mary's Hospital, Pender Harbour, B.C.

Rose often thought about the struggle of being a single parent. She was aware that to nurture a tiny baby you it bathe daily, you admired it, you kissed it, you touched it lovingly, you sprinkled sweet smelling powder on it so that others would want to hold it and love it too. As the baby grew you praised every new skill, until the child grew to independence, loving itself, feeling capable of being a worthwhile person. "But" Rose thought, "Who nourishes the single mother? She needs all these things, too, and there is no one there for her. When a man does enter her life he expects the mother to put his needs before the children. Quite often men are interested only in sex. Certainly not in taking on the responsibility of three young children whose father was 'the other man'."

Chapter 1

"I WILL NOT GET INTO that wet bed with you!"

The matron of the little Pender Harbour Hospital chuckled as she heard the emphatic raised voice of the young nurse coming from the open door of the only single room at the end of the corridor. "Men never give up on certain things no matter how old and decrepit they become," the matron thought. This patient was both old and decrepit.

Just then Rose saw George Haskins come in the door of the hospital. George drove children along the corridor from Halfmoon Bay to the Madeira Park school.

"George, would you and Wynne please see me before you leave the hospital?" she asked.

"Of course," George answered, "I'll see if Wynne is packed up and ready."

Rose was in a thoughtful mood. She was the matron of the smallest hospital in North America. It was listed as having fourteen beds, but they seldom had less than twenty patients. She was the single parent of three young children, David, Kathleen and Gary.

She had struggled to keep her youngsters together, healthy and happy, but now she felt the need to increase her leadership skills to help make her work less stressful.

She has been searching the nursing journals for a suitable course. None were available in Canada but she had found one listed for Loyola University in Chicago for the spring semester. It was called "Principles of Supervision in Nursing" and she could take it in the evenings allowing her to work full time in nursing.

Then Rose searched the journals again until she found a hospital with a nurses' residence, the Cook County Hospital. She had applied and been accepted to start work in January 1959.

Rose wanted to give her children the privilege of living in a home with both a man and wife who cared about each other so that the children could learn the give and take of a normal loving relationship like the one she experienced with the Lowery family at Beaver Mines.

Wynne and George had just lost a much wanted pregnancy. They were depressed. It was not the first and time was running out for them. Rose knew sometimes when people adopted a child the wife soon became pregnant with their own child. She hoped her children would be the solution for George and Wynne as she was genuinely touched by this family's sorrow.

"Here we are," George called. "What can we do for you?"

"Good! I am going to ask a great favour of you. I hope you'll both agree. I need to go to Chicago to take a leadership course. I cannot take the children. Would you take care of them for me?"

George and Wynne looked at each other, then almost in unison they said, "You mean we'll have the kids for Christmas? We would love to have them." And with big smiles, "Can we take them this weekend?"

Rose had not anticipated the children leaving her at the beginning of December but the kids were so thrilled that she agreed. All the necessary financial arrangements were completed, and that week their belonging were packed and off they went, with barely a backward glance at Mom, to the home at Sakinaw Lake. Rose began her preparations to leave for Chicago.

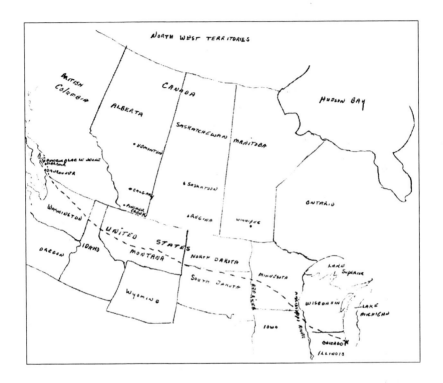

Chapter 2

❦

HISTORY OF ST. MARY'S HOSPITAL: excerpts from "St. Mary's Hospital - the first fifty years, August, 1930 to Sept. 16, 1968."

"St. Mary's Hospital was built on donated land and built by local citizens at the urging of Rev. John Antle, Superintendent of the Columbia Coast Mission and skipper of the mission hospital ship "Columbia". The hospital was named after St. Mary's Church in Kerrisdale whose members generously gave financial and physical help to build it. Two engineers from the church built the hydro electric plant with 100 foot head of power obtained from Garden Bay Lake just above the hospital site. The hospital was opened August 16, 1930 to care for the hundreds of men, women and children living in scattered settlements along the upper portion of the Sechelt Peninsula and on the coasts and islands in and around Jervis Inlet."

Rose had been matron of this fourteen bed hospital for more than a year. It sat on the side of a hill overlooking the beautiful Pender Harbour, said to be the safest harbour on the British Columbia coast.

The hospital was a wooden building two stories high. This concerned Rose greatly as she had been told a fire could destroy it in a very brief time, not only because of the wooden structure but because of the location as well.

The top floor contained a small nursery with windows facing the water. Adjoining this room was a female ward where the maternity patients were accommodated as well as other ladies when necessary. There was a small room containing an adequate but old x-ray machine. A room across the hall was used as an operating room, a delivery room and a wound dressing room, or whatever else it might be needed for. Dr. Playfair had even treated an emergency on a dog in it. Down the corridor were one or two rooms for either sex. At the end was a four bed men's ward. This hospital was listed as a fourteen bed unit but Rose found there were seldom less than eighteen or twenty patients at all times.

The bottom floor contained the kitchen, the staff dining room, the offices of the two doctors as well as a laboratory, pharmacy and a dark room.

Rose's duties were extremely interesting and varied. She was always thankful for the training she had received from the Grey Nuns of the Holy Cross Hospital, Calgary, and the Kahler School of Nursing, Rochester, Minnesota. She was also thankful for all her post graduate experience, including operating room duties in Nelson, B.C. prior to joining the Canadian Army Medical Corps. During World War II she had been stationed both in Canada and overseas. This wealth of experience served her well.

Rose found in Pender Harbour that she was not only in charge of nursing but of pharmacy and laboratory as well. One day, when she was drawing blood up in a pipette by mouth (remember this was a long time ago) a staff member made her laugh and the blood shot into her mouth. Dr. Swan said, "It's O.K., Rose, it only has a few spirochettes in it."

"Thanks a bunch. I'll only get a touch of syphilis I suppose," Rose replied.

Nonetheless, Rose enjoyed every aspect of the job except she tried subtly to avoid having anything to do with the x-ray equipment. She had a thing about rays from the machines. However, one day Dr. Playfair said, "Mrs. White, are you going to learn to take these x-rays?" What Rose heard was, "If you don't start taking the x-rays, forget it. You are gone." With three children to support, she caved in and agreed to this additional duty.

Wasting no time, Dr. Playfair, gave her the instructions that day; how she must wear a lead-lined apron to protect her most sacred areas; how to time the juice; how to position the patient and of course not to forget the film. Then it was downstairs to learn the intricacies of the dark room.

Sometimes Rose found it necessary to go into the laundry on the handyman's day off and wash the diapers for the nursery. This task she loved to do. She hung them outside on the line in a soft, sunny breeze while she admired the view of the harbour and watched the boats coming and going. It reminded her of caring for her own babies in the Alberta sunshine.

There were two doctors at the hospital who had been friends in the Navy in World War II. They were more than competent, they each had a terrific sense of humour and they liked people. Their maternity care was superb because of one standing order: "Do not let the patient bear down until she is fully dilated". This meant that we did not need episiotomies, we never needed a Caesarian section. The only anesthetic was 50 m.m.s of demerol. The mothers were free ot infection and the babies were the healthiest Rose had ever seen in her nursing career.

The operating room, Rose's specialty, was also a joy. The two doctors would operate together while Rose administered the anesthetic. The anesthetic machine, as Rose liked to call it, was an empty coffee can with two round holes about the size of a ten cent piece punched into the lid. Ether was poured into the can and a rubber tube took it to the patient via intubation. The other hole allowed air into the can. In fact it was an excellent method and never caused a problem. Several times doctors from the U.S.A. coming into the harbour in their yachts would see the little hospital on the hill and come for a visit. Rose loved to show them the anesthetic device, much to their delight.

Several times, to her embarrassment, she saw a black fly flitting about the operating room while an operation was being performed. The doctors would say, "Oh! Here is our sterile fly!" It must have been for they never had a post-operative infection.

One day, Dr. Playfair said, "Mrs. White, we will have to operate on John Doe, to take that gangrenous foot off. The gangrene is spreading. I have not been able to get him into a hospital in Vancouver. Do you think we can do it tomorrow?"

Of course. Will ten A.M. suit you?"

Fortunately, Dr. Playfair's father-in-law, a surgeon from South Africa, was visiting Pender Harbour. He had done many leg amputations because of shark bites, so he came into the operating room and directed the two younger doctors and Rose in a technique that was new to them. It was so neat. It was the first time Rose had seen an amputation heal so beautifully, without infection.

Late one summer afternoon, Rose answered a loud banging on the hospital door. An agitated man stood there.

"Quick! Get the doctor! A car has gone into the lake. There are eight people in it. Three are children. Hurry!"

"The doctor can't do much good until we get the people out of the water. I'll phone the pub first to send help."

While Rose was phoning Dr. Swan she heard the zoom, zoom of cars heading to the lake. Dr. Swan soon came to pick up his medical bag.

"May I go with you?" Rose asked.

He was glad to have her. By the time they arrived at the scene, two women, three children and two men had been pulled from that cold mountain lake by friendly young men who had so recently been downing a beer in the warm comfort of the pub. They were just heaving the last person out, a stout man, but it was too late for him. No amount of resuscitation could revive him.

Rose was standing with the women and children. One of the women said, "Too bad. You know, Joe, (the dead man) was driving."

One of the divers said, "It's funny. If Joe was driving, why was he stuck in the back seat?"

Rose thought the woman showed great presence of mind to have figured out so quickly the best way to handle a sticky situation.

The lake where the car went in with eight passengers.

Love and Sex

Love is twenty four hours a day

Sex is five minutes

Love is letting someone grow

Sex is to conquer

Sex without love can beget a baby

Love alone can nourish a child

Sex can begin a marriage

Love alone can nourish it

Sex is now

Love is forever.

Chapter 3

❧

THE MATRON OF A SMALL hospital faces traumatic situations daily, not only with maintaining quality care of the patients, but helping young nurses gain experience. Rose was often heard remarking, "Just call me Ann Landers! " as she also helped staff cope with their personal problems. There was a nurse's residence not far from the hospital. It was quite a nice building. Rose was called there one day by the cleaning lady who had discovered a huge sea turtle in the bathtub. It had been brought in by a nurse for a lark.

The administrator could also be a problem. His main concern is the hospital budget. The lower he keeps it the more secure his well paid position. This can have a severe impact on the number of staff and the amount of equipment and supplies.

Another party concerned with the smooth running of the hospital is the local hospital board. It is made up of members from the community. Rose felt she needed more leadership training to cope with their concerns. Then Dr. Playfair resigned and everything changed. This move finalized Rose's decision to leave

Pender Harbour.

Her last happy day were spent at Sakinaw Lake with her children and with George and Wynne for a dream Christmas by the water. Though the children were sad to see her go, they were full of excitement and plans for the months Rose would be away. She could leave with peace of mind and concentrate on this new adventure.

Chapter 4

❧

ROSE, WHO HAD NEVER BEEN away from her children, missed them that last month in Pender Harbour. For them it was a wonderful new adventure. They took to it "like ducks to water". As she started closing the home they had shared she thought wistfully about the last two years. They had arrived after spending the fall and winter in a cabin at the hunting and fishing resort at Lac Le Jeune near Kamloops where Rose had been a part time cook and general help at the lodge. The children had attended the one room schoolhouse. Their teacher, Mrs. Whittaker, was the wife of the owner of the resort.

It had been a wonderful experience for each of them and their cat, Twinker. Rose remembered seeing David going fishing with a guest from the lodge. She remembered them disappearing into the early morning fog misting over the lake. Rose was not surprised when, waiting on some American guests, a gentleman said with a smile, "You know, that little fellow of yours, Gary, advised us never to go fishing on Lake Okanagan. He said he fished there all one summer and never got a bite."

"I know," Rose answered. "I used to pray he would get one." He was four years old!

The arrival of the family at Lac Le Jeune from Vancouver was the start of a totally new experience. The cook, a middle aged comfortable appearing woman, greeted Rose.

"Are you a registered nurse?"

"Yes," Rose answered.

"Well, you're a goddamned fool," were her next words. With that, she and Rose became good friends.

The little family, including Twinker, were housed that first night in a shed with a covered walkway to another shed. The bed was against the back wall. Everyone slept in it. The children had put a saucer of milk for Twinker outside the door on the walkway. During the night a loud licking sound wakened them. They could hear lots of loud grunting, snorting and shoving as they stared with bated breath at their insecure door. Next morning, they learned seven black bears, including two cubs, had visited their shack. Rose knew that with one shove a bear would have landed in their bed.

Suddenly, the kettle on the stove whistled, interrupting the reminiscing about Lac Le Jeune and orientated her back to Pender Harbour. She answered a call from the hospital before settling down to her cup of tea. As she drank it she wondered if all children were as precious as hers.

She recalled when Twinker was pregnant, and started into labour in her prepared bed. Gary stroked her tummy as her contractions started and she mewed with pain. Kathleen, gazing down at Twinker's contractions and hearing her distressed mewing, said, "When I have a baby I'm having an anesthetic for sure."

Rose smiled as she remembered the day Kathleen came home from school and said, "Mom, all those kids at school are so dumb. I had to tell every one of them where babies come from!" Rose waited for a delegation of parents to appear after that one!

Another afternoon, a few months later, that same daughter

came into the little house behind the hospital when Rose was having a cup of tea at the table with friends. "Mom," she spat out breathlessly, "I know how babies are made."

"Ha!" Rose thought, "Now she knows everything."

"And I know how many times you did it!" her daughter continued, to the delight of Rose's friends.

"You do?"

"Yes, three times."

Rose smiled. "That's right," she said.

Out of the mouths of babes! Rose remembered riding in the front seat of a city bus when David was five. Sitting across from her appearing deep in thought, he asked, "How do babies come out? Do they come out of your mouth?"

David was always an adult, Rose thought. When he was five he had his own paper route in summer at Waterton Lakes... The doctors in Pender would joke in the operating room that David would buy and sell Pender Harbour in a few years.

He was ten, the serious man of the family. He helped the other two to collect empty beer bottles which they stacked on the back porch. This caused Rose much embarrassment when a lady from the church came to call.

One day, when Rose and the children were attending a barbecue at the Klein family, Mrs. Klein said, "Lucky you taught your children what to do in case of fire."

"Why?"

"Didn't David tell you what happened two weeks ago?"

"No."

"Well, we had a fire in our garbage barrel. David's clothes caught on fire. He didn't run. He just laid on the ground and rolled until the fire was out."

The little home behind the hospital that Rose and the children lived in was just a shack with one room barely divided into a small bedroom and a kitchen area. The other nurses lived in the attractive residence up the hill but this was the only available shelter for the matron with children. The clear advantage was that it was very close to the hospital. So close, in fact, that you could hear the mothers when they cried out in labour. Gary often sat in the entrance talking to the expectant fathers as they waited for the birth. He would see the new baby along with them. Although it was not the fashion at that time to let the fathers into the labour room, Rose would have liked to let Gary witness a birth. At this thought she would smile, knowing what an uproar would ensue in the community.

David and Kathleen could already swim, and were soon like dolphins in the water. One day, when Rose came from work into their little home, she found wet shoes on the porch, wet socks and wet trousers in the kitchen, and a wet shirt on the bedroom floor. Looking down on the bed she saw a wet shivering mass. A little boy's voice said, "I know I could have drownded! I was jumping from one boat to another and I fell between them. I went right to the bottom." It wasn't long after that that Gary joined the dolphins, swimming with them across the bay and back.

The fifth member of this family was Twinker, the dearly loved grey striped cat. She followed the children to the school water taxi every morning. She would go aboard, walk around, inspect the boat, then jump off. When the boat came back in the evening she would be waiting on the dock to escort her family home. When Rose visited friends in the senior citizen's housing along the shore in the evening, she would look up and see Twinker looking in the cottage window watching her. When the family were away on a weekend, Twinker would disappear. As soon as they returned, she would come out of the trees to greet them.

"How I will miss all of them, " Rose thought, as the train swept across the U.S.A. Bound for Chicago.

Where they swam

Kathleen
Pender Harbour

Chapter 5

❦

ROSE STRUCK UP A FRIENDSHIP with a young lady from Chicago on the uneventful train journey. This young woman lived in a small home not far from Cook County Hospital. She invited Rose to come to supper the evening of their arrival. As soon as Rose had settled into the nurses' residence on the second floor of this immense plain brick building, she called for a taxi. Waiting outside for it to come alongside, she was stunned to see a negro driver (at that time a negro was nearly unknown in her life). This being her first night in this strange city whose reputation was not unknown even to someone from Pender Harbour, Rose debated whether to get in or whether to forget the whole thing. Then she did get in. The driver was very pleasant and he took her directly to the little house. This was a happy start to her time in Chicago.

January 6, 1959

My dear family, and Wynne and George,

You would never believe my first night here. After settling in, I went to supper with a friend I met on the train. It was a warm, friendly, welcome to a new city. You would never believe the commotion when I arrived back at my room. Looking out of my window I saw motorcycle cops, paddy wagons and police cars circling the nurses' residence in the next block to the hospital.

"For Heaven's sakes," I asked another nurse, "What is going on?'

"Oh," she said, "There was a patient, a prisoner, chained to his bed and he has escaped."

"My God! I hope he doesn't poke his head up. With this lot looking for him he will be a goner!"

Finally, I went to bed and slept while the police circled all night.

I miss you. Today will be my first day in the hospital, perhaps the largest in North America. Imagine, four thousand beds!"

Love to all of you, hugs and kisses
Mom.

January 12, 1959

Dear Family, Wynne and George,

This has been quite a day! All the new nurses were started on a week long orientation course, which means we get to learn a lot about the hospital before we are tossed out to work. Cook County Hospital, a Victorian behemoth, is the largest single hospital in the U.S.A., giving it some staggering statistics. It has more than 4,500 beds; more than 100,000 patients in those beds annually; another 250,000 patients in Fantus Clinic; another 350,000 in its diagnostic clinics. It is easy to see why it has been a prize hospital in the country for internship or residency: by sheer numbers the patients offer a variety of clinical problems unduplicated elsewhere. One resident did tell Rose she wasn't sure her training here would help her in private practice as the patients were so ill she would not know how to treat mild cases of anything.

It was very interesting to learn the administrator is called "The Warden" after witnessing the police surrounding the place last night. Touring the wards, I observed the poverty of the furnishings. Beds are old, old metal cots with peeling paint, thin mattresses and worn covers. The patients were mostly negro or coloured people.

The instructor is very nice. She told us to never ever let a piece of equipment out of the hospital to be mended. "You will find everything is chained or nailed down, we have lost so much equipment to thievery."

The emergency area was an education in itself. There were policemen swarming all over it. "It is always like that here. All the victims of crime, dead bodies, beatings etc. are brought here. It is enough to give anyone nightmares forever!"

I have asked to work in pediatrics to update my skill and techniques in nursing children. Only the sickest kids are admitted, mostly in a coma and unconscious. If they come to admitting, even with a high fever, they receive a cold sponge bath and a shot of penicillin and are sent home.

Must stop this letter now. It is time for my bed. I am sure you will all be bored to death, but I have nothing else to talk about. I miss you all very much. I'm looking forward to your letters full of news about Saginaw Lake.

I love you, Mom. xxxxxxxxxx oooooooooo

Picture of nurses' residence

Presbyterian St. Luke's Hospital
Nurses' residence
Cook County Hospital

January 15, 1959

Dear David, Kathleen, and Gary, Wynne and George,

You must be busy. No letters yet. That's O.K. Soon I know.

I've made a new friend living in the residence like me. She works full time in the emergency so has lots of hair raising tales to tell me each time she comes off duty. Gives me nightmares if it is bedtime.

I have been assigned to the children's treatment room. All the procedures such as drawing blood, dressings, specimens, etc., are done in this room. Consequently, I've learned the proper way to "mummy a child" by wrapping a sheet around him, then the doctor can safely draw blood from the neck area or from the groin.

But enough for this letter. David, I am concerned about your eye and will be waiting to hear all about it. I am feeling good and excited about increasing my nursing skills. All for tonight. A hug and kiss for each of you.

Love,

Mom. xxxxxxxxxx ooooooooo

R.R.I.
Halfmoon bay B.C.
Wed 7, 1954 Jan

Dear Mother

The day befor yesterday Newyears-
eve. Stayed at Michels for Newyears-
eve. The day I got there and I went to
gramps and Michel and I fished
in a waterfall we caught about
30 fish. Next day I gone home and
yesterday I went over to the old
cabin to see if the grouse were ther.
I never saw any until I went to the
side then I saw ones head bobing
up and down I take one shot and
I mist I take a nother shot and
mist again then I hit the grouse
he fell but he was stil aliv but
could not fly. I ran up and grab
its tail fethers I pulled them out
and take another snatch and
grabed its wings. I brouht it
home then I cut of its head. We
have been skating this year.

XXOOXXOOXXOOXXOOX
XOOXXOOXXOOXXOOXXOOXXOOXXOOXXOOXX
OOX
X

Your fr son
Gary

B.C.
R.R.1 Halfmoon bay
fri Jan 9, 1959

Dear Mother

I have received your letter. You have probably received Kathys letter and my letter. The games that we have got sure came in handy. Daivid has gust got bake from town. Right now he is wating to have a game of Parcheesi. I got a star in spelling today. I am going to right to Bertha tonight. I see that you are using my righting paper. I hope to see you soon.

I have got a new lunch kit.

Aunte Dora has sent us a present. So I am going to right a letter to thank her.

I have not got any fish sins you left. But am hoping to getch some in sumer. Kathy has broken our recordplayor. Only the redeo is stil in could condicon. XXOOXXOOXXOOXXOOXX OOXXOOXXOOXXOOXXOOXXOOXXOXXXOOXXOOXXOOXXOOXXOOXXO OXXOOXXOOXXOOXXOOXXOOXXOOXX Your son Gary OOXXOOXXOOXXOOXXOOXXOOXXOOXXOOXXOOXXOOXXOOXXOOXXOO XXOOXXOOXXOOXXOOXXOO

R.R.1.
Halfmoon Bay, B.C.
Wed Jan. 7, 1959

Dear mom -,

I hope you are okey and well. Every things okey here. I love it up here and so does Gary. Although it would be better if you were here.

On Tuesday the bus broke down on the Egmont road so there was no school. It had snowed and we had fun. The pond froze over. We were able to skate for two days, then the ice broke. But we enjoyed it to the fullest while it lasted. Our skates will not fit us next year so I guess we'll sell them. About how much are they worth?

I had Holly up. While she was up it was rainy so we went to Sheashelt. Holly and I ate in Dannys diner. The day after New Years Eve I went to her house.

Today we had to walk up the road at quater to eight in the rain. Our sandwiches were wrecked so Uncle Goerge gave us money for our lunch.

How are Aunt Mayo, Uncle Jock and

Skip?

I am training Poncho to do tricks. He has nearly learned to roll over. I plan to teach him to jump through a hoop. His father knows how to do every thing a dog can do.

We wrote thankyou notes to the folk in Calgary. There is a gale blowing and has been all day. It is twenty after seven now and it hasn't gone done the slightest bit well mabe a bit but thats all.

How is David? I'm glad to hear the operation was successful. We will be glad to have him home. I was glad to hear from you. Well there's not much more thats happened here so I guess this is goodbye for now.

Love from Your daughter,
Kathleen.

XXOOXOXO
XOXOXO

P.S. Write as soon as you receive my letter. Love again and forever.

1

R.R.1 Halfmoon Bay
Tues Jan 20/59

Dear Mary:

Thanks so much for you last two letters which until now we have not had an opportunity to answer.

All is well here - your charming little heart stealers are all in the very best of health. This early to bed early to rise seems to agree with them.

I have received the cheque from Mrs. Reild - forgot the other $5.00 - we are being rewarded more than amply be having three lovely children to brighten our lives. I only wish we were in a financial position to keep them without any money from you.

2

The family allowance cheque for Dec and January arrived yesterday - this will be spent on clothing or other essentials for the children.

We are pleased with the progress the children are making in their school work. Kath and David have needed very little help but with some carefully chosen praise we are attempting to spur them on to even greater achievements. Gary is making rapid strides in his spelling and arithmetic with about an hour a day homework. He has now earned three stars for spelling and is as proud as punch.

We are still thoroughly enjoying the children and make every effort to push back the thought of how empty our lives will be without them.

3

We have been working hard on the new house and feel sure we are going to be very comfortable there. It thrills us to hear the children refer to it as "Our new house". They have certainly adapted themselves wonderfully.

David's eye appears to me to be in perfect alignment now however he feels that he will need still another operation. We are arranging to have the Buckley's and Mrs. Murphy take him down with them on the Friday after school and I am sure they will see him right out to Mayo & Jock's

We are working hard trying to remove some of the "Harbour" lingo from their grammar. At the moment we are endeavouring to stem the constant use of "Never". After everything else failed we find the deduction (or threat of,)

4

of one cent from the allowance for every misuse of the word is having the greatest effect.

Enclosed is another gem created by our Gary. You might wonder how he can manage to get a star in spelling but I suppose the implementation of knowledge learned comes with time.

Dear Mary

This is just a note at the end of Georges letter. I hope you had a pleasant trip & are getting into the swing of things there. The children are very well & happy. David has a bit of a cold but very slight. Gary was at Cubs tonight & tells us he gets his scarf tomorrow. The children have all forced us to join the P.T.A. So we attended a meeting the other night.

The children all have bright rosy cheeks and are eating more all the time. For breakfast this morning Kathy had bacon, 1 egg, a good helping of fried potatoes a slice of toast & jam & two glasses of milk. Gary ate more but David omited the toast. But they have a long time to go before lunch. We certainly enjoy the children. Its just as if they had always been here. Well more the next time. We will all write in a day or so. Love from all of us.

Wynne & George.

Dear Mom

I am sorry I did not write sooner, but I have a sprained wrist. The doctor said that I would have to have another operation but not for a while. I have to go down again in five weeks. Everything is fine here how is it at your end. The record player might be able to be fix-ed but if it isn't we get our money refunded. The other day Gary and I saw some muskrat " is now a scout and is quite proud. Aunt Wynne had her sister from Langley her Kathleen is writing a letter also and I imagine you have read it. I went bowling and got 82. I saw one show in town (The buccneer) and one show here (Uncle Remous) I went to a basket ball game at Gibbsons also, danced and talked with Bertha at a party. She was glad to hear you were settled. What is your address? I am building a chicken pen, and work on the house is coming nicely

Yours Son
David.

Sakinaw Lake
RR1 Halfmoon Bay
British Columbia

A FRIEND DAVID
MADE IN LAC LA JEUNE
(MOM)
Jan. 3.

Dear Dr. Shook

Thank you for the lovely card
We have moved about 10 mi. from
Pender Harbour. To a place called
Sakinaw Lake. There is lovely trout
fishing the trout average from
2-4 lbs. There is a good Salmon
spot not to far away. The salmon
average from 10 to 49 lbs. I know
several spots for I am a fish guide.
If you come I can get a boat and
cabin if you still have not got the
trailor truck. If you have I can
still provide facilities. If you want
to come and have not made other
plans I will give you directions on
how the reach me. I have lost your
address and would like you to
send it to me. I am spending this
in care of Post Master General.

Dave White
P.S Thank you for the stamps.
PPS I Just had an successful
operation on my eyes.

B.C.
R.R.1 Halfmoon bay

1

Dear Mom

David and I went out fishing today. We didn't get a thing. But we saw 13 otter. We are building our chiken coop today to. David went out fishing on Wedneday. He had a fish on but it got away. I have learned my 7,5,6,11,2,3,10, times tabl.

2

and only have my 9,8,1 timestabl to learn.

We have had drosy days hear. First we had snow and Uncle Goearch couldn't get the truck the up the hill, then the rain came. Today, and is suppostto rain tomorow to. Kathey went to Holly lions for Saterday and Sunday. Steve is getting a BB gun for his berthday. Last Saterday we went to the show. coled Song of the South. Then last night we went to a basketball game. And got home at 12, oclock thast night, today we packed in a hole tree and staked it in a pile

3

At the basked ball game Uncle Georg and Dok Stonyear ruferred the game. We met Billy Greffsht he told me to say hello the next time I wrote you a leter. There were three men up fishing and they got 3 twenty four inches long. Aunte win, went out fishing but she didn't get anything. We went over to the new house and did some work on it. David run the automatic timer at the basket boll game. One of the girls got so mad that she started to kidked and trampeld

4

We have reseved your letter. I am going to get my cub scarf this Tuesday at cubs. I went over to Akalus house at lunch hour. to pas my test. Chairli, Brini, Kenny all have there skarf This morning I saw a duck and it had a brownish black back a black head and white winges. Last night David and I poped some popcorn, Aunte Win and Uncle Geog went out last night.

5

The sun is coming out this morning. David got a cold and I got one now to. All of the chocolates are gon now. Last Sunday Kathy and I went and got about twelv bullrushes. This morining I'll probably will be going out fishing. We stile have nuts left in the bole. We only us the fireplace at night now. Some men came up to look at lackesls properdy. Will we were working on the new house.

6

David found some root beer under the house so we will probably will be having some today. Aunte win and Uncle Georg, Smoke, Ranky, Ronchy, are all stile in bed and sleaping, Kenny got the flew and was sike in bed with a high fevr. He wasen't at school for 2 or 3 days. Today if Kethy gets home before dark I am going to ask if we can take the benokulers out and look at the otters, David is going out to cut some wood, Twinker, is have a wonderful time hear she goes out hunting with me and she folses us every

7

place we go dar nere. She is bumping her head aganst the pen that is whe my writing isent so good. She has lost her sink now, I got a new par of runing shoes. Twinker has sarp teeth I just had expereence. I hope you liked your trip to Cikago. I have not shot any roeuss yet but as sone as the come bak I will get one. I help with the dushes now. The Blew Gaes are back now. I staked at lest 150 peces of wood last night. It is ten after eleven and they just woke up. Daivrd has got the front of the chiken coop done.

8

Kathy is back now She seaid that she had a good time at the basket ball game and a good time a lions. Uncle Goerg and I tried to get the truk out of the dich.

SWAIK means sealed with a loving kiss.

R.R.1
Halfmoon Bay. B.C.
Wed. Jan 9, 1958

Dear mom,

I'm sorry I didn't wrote sooner but I just didn't have time. With getting home 3:30 then training Poncho and being challenged and challaging to play games. I hope you will forgive me. I have been lonesome too. I walk down the hill instead of going into Egmont after school. So I get home earlier. Auntie Dora and the family got me two collars for wearing with sweeters and blouses. One was white rabbit fur, one pink velvet. They are both pretty. I was glad to get them for I have many sweeters and blouses. Gary has a jackknife that they gave him. David reached home with the letter you wrote. It is still blowing but not as hard. Not anything unusual happened today. How are you and Aunt Mayo, Uncle Jock & dog?

Lovingly yours,
Kathleen.

P.S. Have a nice time
XOXOXOXO
XOXOXOXO

Our sign at top of the road.

George and new boat.

Haskins Seniors',
We all spent winter there.

Our float with some of the boats.

Chicago, January 27, 1959

Dear Gary, Kathleen, David, Wynne and George,

Oh boy! The jackpot! So many lovely long letters. I can't tell you how much I enjoy them amongst all the sickness I see here. They are a breath of fresh air. I especially like how happy you sound.

Sorry to hear the record player is on the fritz. Imagine actually seeing muskrats in the wild! By now I bet you've finished the chicken pen. See all the things you are learning.

I never knew there were so many otters in Sakinaw. I have only seen them in the Stanley Park zoo. Aren't you lucky!

I am proud you're learning your times tables and getting your cub scarf. It is good to know there are fish in the lake, not like in the Okanagan when you fished all summer at Naramata and never got a bite.

Kathleen, skating on the pond reminds me when I was young. Isn't it wonderful to skate outdoors. It was kind of Aunt Wynne to let Holly come for a visit. I am sure you thanked her. Bet you will soon have Poncho the best trained dog in Pender Harbour.

Glad to hear from George and Wynne and to know you are just as happy and having just as much fun as I am.

I miss you all and i love you more than you can know.

With lots of hugs and kisses, XXX XXX XXX OOO OOO OOO

Mom.

STATE OF ILLINOIS, OTTO KERNER, GOVERNOR
DEPARTMENT OF REGISTRATION AND EDUCATION, SPRINGFIELD
1961   THIS IS TO CERTIFY THAT   1962

MARY M. WHITE   41-93575

206 Sandringham Ave.   9X
New Westminster
British Columbia, Canada

IS A

REGISTERED PROFESSIONAL NURSE

EXPIRES   APR 28'61 ISSUED 48,260
5-1-62

ATTEST: WITNESS MY HAND AND SEAL OF SAID DEPARTMENT

Superintendent of Registration   Director

COOK COUNTY SCHOOL OF NURSING
CHICAGO, ILLINOIS

Signature Identification Card
THIS CARD IS ISSUED TO IDENTIFY EMPLOYEE

WHITE, MARY M.   56239

"m. 195 6M. 4-57 F.P.

Chapter 6

❦

Dear Kathleen, David and Gary,

Thank you again for your letters. You are all so good about writing.

I enjoy hearing about all the things you do. Even though we miss each other I feel you are getting a wonderful chance to live in a happy home with people who really like children. I enjoyed that opportunity when I lived on a farm with a lovely English family so that I could start school when I was nine years old.

Imagine, I made it to downtown Chicago today. I bought a few things which I will mail to you. On the way home I got lost. I must have got off at the wrong stop. I was pretty nervous as there were mostly black people everywhere. One tall black man came up to me, stuck out his hand, opened it and said, "Do you want to buy this diamond ring?" Before I could get over my surprise he was gone. Believe me, I was glad to find my way home safely.

I expect my letters are quite boring for you with all these medical things? I feel so sad for all my little patients. Some have a disease I had never heard about before. It is called "Sickle cell anaemia". It is quite common to negro people. The red cells of their blood are shaped like a sickle (gardening tool - George can tell you) and their blood practically turns to water. It is a very painful disease, especially in their joints.

You can't help but love all the kids. They are so cute to look at and usually so good natured. They have big smiles and they love to tease the nurses. They especially please the negro nurse aides who do much of the actual care. I really enjoy watching these women work. They are so patient, kind and gentle - born nurses.

I am not crazy about the two white ladies who work in the kitchen. They passed a very rude remark about Abraham Lincoln who was from Illinois and became President of the United States. He is credited with freeing the negro slaves. I was surprised and upset by their remarks.

The equipment in their kitchen is old and decrepit. There is an old rusty two plate gas burner. Every afternoon about two thirty there are two big opened tins of canned peas sitting there heating until supper time, about four thirty. It seems to me that every supper time the kids get cottage cheese and peas. Believe it or not, they train hundreds of dietitians in this hospital. How I wish the kids could have the wonderful food Mrs. Sundquist cooked in

St. Mary's Hospital, Pender Harbour. Poo on the dietitians!

I will be waiting for your letters. All for now. As always, lots and lots of love and hugs and kisses.

Mom.　xxx　xxx　xxx
　　　　ooo　ooo　ooo

Rose was learning more every day about sickle cell anaemia, as there were so many cases on this unit. Mostly the children were admitted in crisis. The disease can give acute abdominal pain, painful swelling of the soft tissues of the hands and feet, migratory recurrent or constant joint pain with limited movement. There is often persistent headaches, dizziness and convulsions. There can be visual or auditory disturbances, facial nerve palsies, coughing and shortness of breath. Crisis is very painful with a sudden drop in haemoglobin levels when large quantities of blood suddenly accumulate in the spleen causing spleen enlargement, severe anaemia, shock and death.

Rose did not witness a death. Her job was to mummy the patient in the treatment room so the doctor could draw arterial blood either from the neck but preferably from the groin. One little boy begged the doctor, "Don't kill me, doctor, please don't kill me!" Rose wondered what stories he had heard to frighten him so badly.

The treatment for the patient was bed rest, good nursing care and blood products. Rose found the treatment very similar to treatment for leukaemia in Canada.

R.R.1. Halfmoon Bay,
Jan. 26, 1959. B.C.

Dear Mom,

How are you keeping. I was glad
to receive your letter. Please excuse
writing. I am sending you the nicest
picture I did of the two. I hope you
like it. I am always happy to here
from you. How do you like your
room? Do you like your job. I hope
you do. Did you have a nice time
on the way? I have passed all my
tests so far. I hope you are glad to
here. In fact I know you are.

The boys are working on the chicken
coop. I walk down the hill every day
after school. We have got a lot done
on the house now. Poncho knows
how to sit up. I don't know if I
told you that before or not. There's
not much happed round here so
my letter isn't very long.

We saw the show in Gibsons of
Uncle Remus. It was really good. I
stayed at Hollys over the weekend.
We had loads of fun. Well my arm
aches so I will have to close. bye for
now.

                    Your daughter
                    Kathleen.

P.S.
I wasn't feeling well but I'm fine

now. Hope you are too.
XOXOXOXO
XOXOXO
XO "over"

SWALK

Dear Mom,

I recieved you letter and I'm sure Uncle George will phone. My report cards marks are good. The are as follows

General Marks

Language	C	N	— WORK HABIT
Spelling	C	G	
Reading	B	G	
Writing	B	N	
Arithmatic	C		
Science	C+	N	
Social S	C+	G	
Art	pass		
Phys Ed.	C+	N	
Health etc.	P	P	

It was a pretty good report wasn't it. Mother I miss you terribly we pray for you every night hopping things will turn out. I think my eyes will be all right. I am glad you got your passport and everything is turning out. I'm did not fly in. I was glad to here from you. There has been sevral storms the floats broke looss and we are looking for a boat now.

Yours Truly David

XXXX OOOO

R.R.1 Halfmoon Bay, B.C.
Monday Jan. 26, 1959

Dear Mary,

Just a note to say that I have forwarded Jim the full details of the property you were interested in, today.

I dropped down to Halfmoon Bay today and saw the owner. He said the property was still for sale although someone was interested and was to let him know about it this week. He indicated he would accept terms and was asking $2700.00 I suggested to Jim that the property was in my opinion worth considerably more than the asking price and highly recommended it as a good buy.

Gary was quite perturbed when he looked for his letter he was writing to you and said I had mailed it. He stated in rather horrified voice that he had not finished the letter, hadn't even signed his name to it - - - "How" he wanted to know "would you know who it was from". We assured him that even if you did not recognize his handwriting you would certainly connect the spelling with none other than our boy.

He is doing much better with his spelling and his arithmetic and I am hoping that with some effort we can get that exceptionally good brain of his to concentrate on such mundane things as spelling and arithmetic.

We were under pressure from all sides and let Kath go in to visit with Holly on the week end but have advised her that she can't go again for a long time. I personally don't think it does her any harm mentally but the kids stay up far too late at night and she comes home all tired out and on the verge of getting sick. Another month and we hope to be in our own house and have room for the kids to entertain their friends here which we much prefer. We noticed that one week end away can undo about three weeks of grammer and manner training we have put forth here.

Dave leaves on Friday night for town and we are hoping that his eye is as good as it appears to us, in which case he will be right home.

Must dash now, enclose two more letters for you.

Love,

R.R.1 Halfmoon Bay B.C.
Monday Jan 26/59

1

Dear Mom

I got 5 X out of 38 woards that I did not get a chants to study the words I went out and dumped the garbage. I didn't get a chanch to adres my last letter, becase Uncle Goareg take it and put it in an envelop and it was sent to you. I have still got my B,Bs that I got 3 weeks and one day Kathey and I are sending away for books. We have all read the books that we got for Christmas from you.

2

I knew my 8, Times and my 9 times now I have only my 12 times to learn. I knew all my spellings. We are having a big test. Whene are our sunday school papers coming? We had rain againe today. We had a Language test and I think I got 100 % persent.

R.R.1. Halfmoon Bay
Wed 14, 1959

Dear Mother

Im tring to get my 2 star in
spelling today I got a hair kut. It is
the first one I have ever liked. I gust
got 5 new pakets of BBs today and
new runners I have been out of
BBs for a week. I am going to Cubs
againe. Chairly, Kenny and Brin
have all got thir hole uniform. I
got my last poleo shot today. Wene
will ever sunday school papers get
her David has beet uncle Jorg in a
game of crib and Kathy has beet
aunt win in a game of chekers
and I beet aunt win in a game
of chekers. I have not got any fish
yet. X X O O X X O O O X O X O O O X O X O X O O O X O X O O X O
X O X O X O O X O
X X O X X O X O X O X O X O X O X O X O X O X O X O X O X O X
O X O X O X O X O X O X X O X O X O X O O
                                                You son Gary
X O X O X O X O X O X O X O X O X O X O X O X O X O X O X O X O
X O
X O X O X O X O X O X O X O X O X O X O X O X O X O X O X O X O
X O   X O X O X O X O X O X O X O X O X O X O X O X O X O X O X
O X O X O
X O X O X O X O X O X O X O X O X O X O X O X O X O X O X O X O
X O
X O X O X O X O X O X O X O X O X O X O X O X O X O X O X O X O
X O
X O O X X O

R.R.1 Halfmoon bay B,C.
Tues 15, 1959

Dear Mother

I got a star in spelling today
and are hoping to get another star
tomoro. The dogs are getting ust of
us now. And the kats are getting
ust of each other. We arn't having
very could wether her. I hope you
will have a nice trip to Chicago.
We are having foun hear. In the
wind ferst the flout flouted away
then the sailboat flouted away. We
had two pitcher shows at school.
One was about loging Qubec. The
next was abot how mony is made.
Aunte Win and Uncle Gorg have put
in the bathroom sink in the new
house. I got a star in arithmetic
today. I see you are using the
righting paper that I gave you for
Christmas. XoXoXoXoXoXoXoXoXoXoXo
XoXoXoXoXoXoXoXoXoXoX
XoXoXoXoXoXoXoXoXoXoXoXoXoXoXoXoXoXo
XoXoXoXoXoXoXoXoXoXoXoXoXo

Your son Gary

XoXoXoXoXoXoXoXoXoXoXoXoXoXoXoXoXoXo
XoXoXoXoXoXoXoXoXoXoXoXoXo
XoXoXoXoXoXoXoXoXoXoXoXoXoXoXoXoXoXo
XoXoXoXoXoXoXoXoXoXoXoXoXo

Dear Mom.

Thank you for the valentine and pensils we have been busy fishing. Jim Flue in and Larry is going to make an offer. I am studying ancient egypt witch is quite facinatin I splite quite a bit of wood tonight. We had a lovely dinner of roast pork, turnips collyflour, New Potatoes and gravy. We worked on the new house and Aunt Wynne said we might be in by Easter. I nailed all the tar-paper on an a bit of planking. I hope things are all well down their. I hope you get used to the climat soon. Gary I guess as he will tell you he caught a fish 2 lb 1 ounce. I caught one the day before which weighed 1 lb. I went to a basketball game at Gibson-s friday and went to a show called the Gypsy colt.

I saw Anne Robinson and Billy Griffith and said hello to them for you. They all ask me about you. Billy said, "I didn't know where your mother was and was going to drop of and see her." I am always thinking about you and hoping we get the property and evrything works out.

Your loving Son

David White

P.S.

Write soon, there is wax on the paper and my pens skipping

ooooooooooooooooooooooooooooooooooooooooo
ooooooooooooooooo

xxxxxxxxxxxxxxxxxxxxxxxxxxxxxxxxxxxx
xxxxxxxxxxxxxxxxxxxx

1

R.R.1. Halfmoon Bay
Feb 3, 1959. B.C.

Dear Mom;

I hope you are feeling well. I love you and I think about you all the time. We got a letter from Bertha. I miss you just awful its been awfuly lonesome without. I hope you like it there. I, will write oftener from now on. I would like to write everyday but we have been studing for our tests. I passed all my tests. I plan to work even harder though and get even better yet. Gary has improved greatly in his work. In our problem test I got Excellent. I'm sorry I didn't send my ballia pictures, but aunt Whin said it would bend if it didn't have a frame. We haven't got our reports yet but expect them soon. I have started to teach Poncho to jump through the hoop. I feel it will be his hardest to learn but he'll learn. I know! I hope you feel fine. Have you heard from Jim lately. I'm sorry you don't receive our letters sooner than you do.

2

How are you feeling well. We have just marked our langauge tests, but Mr. Freeman has to do a bit more on them yet. I have been invited to Carols this weekend. I'm sure we'll have fun. Have you made any new friends in Chicago yet. (excuse my spelling.) I bailed out a boat so we have two to row in now. Hope you're having a nice time. Are you? I think those rocky mountain goat glass stirrers are real neat. I'm sending you all my money. That is what's left. I bought a pink hair band and I think its pretty. With my money I want you to buy me a pretty skirt or dress size 11 or 10 1/2. Aunt Wynne is going to let me cook the meal tomorrow. I'm going to have pie, sausages, fried potatoes, corn green beans I've asked her to teach me to cook and sew. She said she would. bye for now

Your daughter
Kathleen.
with lots of
love and kisses

X O X O X O   X O O O
X O X O X O   X O O O
X O X O X O   X X X X
X O X O X O   X O O O

Dear Mom,

A top student in school got 7 out of 19 and I got 16 out of 19. I got a fish on today that I could not reel in it was so big. I Played in a basketball com on Friday I also went to one on Tues.

Mr. Goldrup got 14 fish today. Our room on the new house will soon be finished. When Larry was killed and there was a missing person we were sure it was Jim both Larry and Jim flew in and said that Uncle George could make an offer on the property But yesterday Jim phoned and said the offer still stands. We had cold chicken and potatoe salid for supper. We got the new licence plates on the buses. Kathleen is going to make a skirt out of pretty material. We were in Garden Bay yesterday, and They are working on the hospital. Everyone asks me how you are and how " " getting along. The days ae flying by and it won't be long until we're togeather

Your Son
david

P.S. Hope you get used to the weather.

Feb the 5 have not got any fish yet. I have got 6.25 saved up now. Kathy ods has 15 and some not 50 cents. Darro has not save anything. Aunte Win and Uncl Goarag has are going out tonight. We have made red and white

Valatine. One Saterday I cooked breakfast and lite the fire. Smoke went out of the house and came back and a skunk had sprad him. Darro is tring to teck how to play. Aant Win and Uncl Doug are you haven got the foundabahons down.

Feb the 5

Darry X

R.R.1
Halfmoon bay
Wed 5, 1959

Dear Mom
I past 9 tests and are improving in writing. I have got my skarf and 3 bdages to.

I am going to stay at Michels place on Sat we are going to slep in the hay. I think Ima goise to pao We are o going to get our report. It is halling hear,

Feb the 5

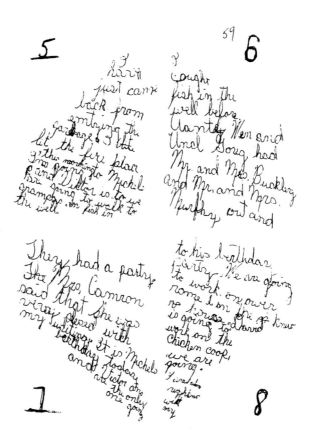

R.R.1 Halfmoon Bay B.C.
April 6, 1959

Dear Mom

We got our school pictures today but I gave mine to the teacher because she didn't get one. We went to a show we saw it before but it was worth seeing it it was the show of 2 thousand leges under the sea. I caught steel heads.

p.g. 9

Dear Mom

I just got back from Michels house. I caught about 15 fish. Michels caught about 15 to. When we got home Victor left befor we did because he tosed rocks at the sike calf. And was going to get in truble. Michel and I walked a mile or 2. We foald I or 2 squeils home, there was about 10 or 20 trees and under the trees there was about a foot or two of these thing from the akorns under each tree. We foand a cave that was longer than me.

Snuffy could go in the cave head first and come out head first so it must get wider at the end. Then when we coming home a truk came along then. Sunny came along. On Thursday I got a star in spelling. Our sunday school papers have been ariving. Kathy is darning her soks now and I am getting the kindling. Uncle Goerg bot a now car and he is taking it apart. David and Uncle Goerg are having a game of krib. I found my woggle. Aunt Win is reading. Twinker is going to have kittens soon and we are going to drown them. We are going to go to a high

school play tomorrow night. I
think I am going to get a star in
a reading test.
XOXOXOXOXO Your Son Gary
XOXOXOXOXOXOXOXOXO

Dear Mary:

Just a note to accompany the childrens letters.

Jim and Larry flew in about one P.M. On Friday and I took them on a "Cooks tour" of the property. I knew Jim was sold so I concentrated my remarks and selling effort on Larry. If you know Larry you will understand when I say I couldn't be sure if he liked the place or thought as we all do that Laskso's property was a good buy. After walking over it, seeing the cabin, the location of corner posts etc. and then walking over as far as our new place and back we ended up sitting in our place looking at maps when Larry suggested to Jim the he (Jim) have me contact Laskso and make him a cash offer for the place of $1500.00. Jim suggested they be prepared to go up to $2000.00 but Larry felt I should

2

stick at the $1500.00 offer then phone him and let him know how I made out.

We are going to see Laskso on Wednesday and will do our best to get him to accept, however I don't really think he will take $1500.00 or even $2000.00 but he might. One thing about starting low with $1500.00 is that it makes the $2000.00 look a lot better. The biggest hope I have is that Laskso's poverty might influence him in accepting. Even at $2500.00 I think it is a bargain.

Will let you know the moment we find anything definit.

Will leave the gossip to Wynn so will close now with fondest regards & the hope all is going well with you down there.

Sincerely
George

Chapter 7

❧

Chicago, February 2, 1959

My dear family and Wynne and George,

Thank you for your letters. I am glad Gary is doing so well with his spelling and times tables. Don't worry, Gary, I knew which letter was yours. Those Sunday school papers should start coming soon. Let me know.

Dave, your report was a good one. I am proud of you. I know you will be a big help to Uncle George on the new house. I will be waiting to hear about your eyes. Before you know it I will be home again. Even though it is sad to be apart, I needed to get this leadership training and there was nowhere in Canada where I could work full time and go to school.

Kathleen, thank you for the picture. You do

have talent. I did enjoy relaxing on the train. I met a nice lady from Chicago so we travelled together. My room is very plain but comfortable. I've made friends with a nurse who works in County Emergency. She tells me some hair raising tales about people who come through her department. Sometimes it is hard to sleep afterwards, especially if she tells me at bedtime. Sure not like the hospital at Pender Harbour. It will be fun for you when Holly can come to Sakinaw to spend overnight with you.

When I was at work today I got a surprise. I was standing at the treatment room door waiting for my next patient when I saw a doctor hurrying down the hall. I heard the head nurse holler after him, "You can go to Hell! I will not give that medication. If you want to kill the patient YOU give it!"

Wow" I had never in my life thought I would hear a nurse talk like that to a doctor. I was kind of tickled. I suspect it will have a profound effect on my nursing from now on. You see, we were taught that the doctor was next to God and never wrong.

One of the housekeepers in the nurses' residence told me a nurse has two bedrooms on our floor. In one she has fish tanks all around, full of goldfish. She has them all named and spends lots of time talking to them. She has been here many years. Oh well! I spend my time writing to you.

Goodnight. God bless you all.

xxx xxx xxx ooo ooo ooo

With lots of love, Mom.

Chapter 8

❦

THE DAYS WERE FULL OF surprises, with new types of patients and always educational experiences for Rose who soaked it all up like a sponge.

There were severe cases of lead poisoning, something she had never encountered in Canada. She was told the poor children ate the plaster powder from holes in the walls of the tenement buildings. The plaster had lead in it. Her only prior experience with this type of poisoning happened when she was a child. Her father's favourite colt died from convulsions from lead poisoning which it got from licking the paint from the fence in front of their log cabin.

The following are some interesting statistics:

Degree of urbanization	Race	
	White	Black
Urban, 1,000,000 persons or more	4.0	15.2
Central City	4.5	18.6
Non-central city	3.8	3.3
Urban, less than 1,000,000 persons	1.6	10.2
Rural	1.2	10.3

From Mosby's Medical & Nursing 2nd edition page 1037

The children who were admitted to her area were very ill, and generally in a coma. The lead poisoning caused their condition. They had persistent vomiting, drowsiness, incoordination that could end in paralysis, convulsions and coma. Their gums became discoloured with lead levels in bones and hair and blood.

Intelligence was lowered with a diminished attention span. They were treated with a chelation therapy. When administered, the lead in the body bonded with the chelation agent and was excreted in the urine.

Rose had never seen or taken care of deformed babies and children. At that time in B.C. Most of these little ones were placed very soon after birth in such places as Woodlands, a care facility in New Westminister B.C. In the children's ward at Cook County she was saddened to see every possible kind of malformation. She found the negro aides were superb nurses of these children. One little child had been born with no eyes or any sign of them. Another had one eye just above the bridge of the nose. Some of these children were born to syphilitic parents.

While Rose was there, a little girl about nine years old was brought in by her family. She had an enormous head and a very small body. Rose had only seen one other like her in a circus when she was a child. That little person had been in a cage and not very clean. However, this little girl in Chicago, although from a poor family, had been beautifully cared for. Her skin was in perfect condition. It had taken excellent nursing care at home to keep her this way. It was her very first time in any hospital.

Rose did not realize that, in spite of her appearance, the little girl's mind might be the same as yours and mine. A few hours after her family had left, something sad in her face caught Rose's eye. "Hello, Christine. You look sad. Are you lonely for your family?" Two large tears rolled down the little girl's face, and her mouth trembled. Rose was shocked. Never again would she underestimate the ability of any patient to understand those around them. Christine had taught her a valuable lesson.

To mom,

Sorry to hear you aren't feeling well with your throat. Hope it isn't as hot as they say this summer. I can wear my hair in a pony tail again now. We had our pictures taken today that is class pictures. Yesterday our single pictures were taken. When we get them I will send them to you. I had a good report but I think I could have done better. Garys class had six dollars stolen. Glenna said when she was with June, June went into her room and took money out of Mrs. Camrons desk but I don't know if its true or not. I would love to see your ward but oh well. Our room on the new house is nearly finished. We might move in, in the Easter holidays. We're not sure though. My valentine won't be here on time so sorry to be late. There is a gale blowing now. It was snowing today but not much. I have darned hearts in a pair of socks for valentines day. And my initials in another pair.

Lots of love
Kathy

P.S. Glad you like your apartment
XOXOXO
XOXOXO

R.R.1 Halfmoon Bay
Feb 20, 1959

Dear Mom

David and I both got a fish mien weigh 1 pound and 10 ounces. David weigh about 3 corters of a pound. I have gand my apitit now. Kathy and I rode 6 miles in the back of the truk. The grous have not came back yet put the fishing is good. Uncle Gorg has a sweter it is red and white. Jim was up and he looked at the properdy and he said that he was going make a pargan. We have arived your letter and the fan, pencils. Have you bot my B.B. Gun scope. We have not had much time to right to you. I mad a cat at the new house. It looks like this. Aunte Win is reading the book of Swiss family Robinsion we are at where they are at the ship.

Aunt Win and Uncle Goreg have got the Gyp-rocking don on our room. Last night we went to the show of The Gippsey colt it was about a horus. I will tell you wate it was about. This colt allwes came to school and piged up a girl at school She was about 9. It hadn't raind for 2 years and the colt had to drink water and there wasn't anof water so they had to sell the colt. This horus tranor bot the colt It was time for school to be out. The girl saw the go past the school. Continue tomorrow.

Your Son Gary

XO ooo×oo××o××oo××oo××ooxx

R.R.1 Halfmoon Bay
Feb. 20, '59 B.C.

Dear Mom,

How have you been feeling. Sorry to hear about your throat. Glad to hear about the negro children. You must be having fun with them. You draw cute pictures. Gary and I rode to the garage in the back of the truck when we were going to the garage to get the school bus. It was sure fun. We received the pencils, fan and coasters. Sure think the pencils are cute. The fan is sure pretty. And oh, the Rockey Mountain goat bar stirrers came too. But I thought you knew so I didn't tell you sooner.

We went to the show Gypsy colt. I'm sure I've seen it before though! It was sad in parts but was still good. We had trout for supper yesterday it was sure good. Miss you lots. We got the valentines but they were a day late. Sure are neat. We're saving them for next valentines day. Did you receive my valentine please tell me. I baked cookies today. They turned out good.

We got some more gip rocking up in our room. (excuse my writing pen skips) Aunt Wyne is reading

us Swiss family Robinson. Gee
its good. Our teacher is reading
us Coral Island. I must go now!
Bye. Love you forever and ever. Love
you.

From your loving
daughter lots of it,
Kathleen White

P.S. Write soon as usual. How is
your friend what is her name.

Mar 6th

Dear Mom,

Gary went fishing when it was raining very hard and caught 2 fish one 3 1/4 lbs the other 1 5 lb. He caught them in 15 min. Kathaleen is now making a dress Gary is painting a picture given to him by the Haskins. I might have a chance to play in a basketball game on the 14th. Mrs. Flemming said that I had improved grately. We have two skunks but they're got to go. I will write you more tomorrow.

Water Tower Campus

WATER TOWER CAMPUS: Part of Chicago's "Magnificent Mile," this campus is named for the landmark the Water Tower, across the street. Located on the "Gold Coast," Chicago's most elegant residential neighborhood, the Water Tower Campus is just a few minutes from the center of the banking, communication, and commercial

industries and just a few blocks from quaint galleries, world-renowned museums, and designer boutiques. A truly ideal address, you'll find many of the city's riches at your classroom door.

71 A

MISSION
- Loyola University Chicago is a national, independent, urban university in the Jesuit Catholic tradition. Loyola is dedicated to higher education and health care, emphasizing excellence in teaching, research, and community service. The Jesuit tradition, as embodied at Loyola, focuses on the development of the individual student, including intellectual, social, and spiritual growth within the Judeo-Christian framework.
- Loyola's goal is to teach, heal, and serve others as a contribution to the glory of God and to impart to its students, patients, faculty, and employees the importance of living lives that express the values they embrace.

FOUNDED 1870

Lake Shore Campus

The oldest and largest of the two undergraduate campuses, Lake Shore Campus hugs the shore of Lake Michigan in a residential community on Chicago's north side. Set in 48 acres of landscaped grounds, Lake Shore Campus serves as home for more than 4,000 undergraduate students in the College of Arts and Sciences, the School of Education, and the Nichoff School of Nursing.

LAKE SHORE CAMPUS

Chapter 9

A lovely thing is dignity -
To move among no matter
what fine forms of sod
With this significant equality
That I, too, hold my being
straight from God.

Elsie A. McDowall (about 1935)
Beaver Mines, Alberta

Something happened in this leadershp course to change forever how Rose viewed democracy.

There were thirty nurses in the class, three were negro nurses. They were all from different areas keen to improve their skills as supervisors, head nurses and team leaders.

"Welcome to Loyola and to this class. The first thing I want you to do is to write an essay on all you know about democracy," the instructor said.

"This should be easy," Rose thought. "I come from a democratic country. Let me think now. Oh, yes! Freedom, that's the big thing. We are free to do anything we want, to become anything we want. We are free to say anything we want. We have a secret vote to elect our government. What else? There has to be more than that bit."

Try as she might, Rose could not think of anything else for the essay. She was embarrassed. She was to learn just how limited her informaton was that she had learned going through the Canadian school system.

The instructor gathered the papers, then said, "I want you to think of democracy and responsibility. When you live in a democratic society you have responsibilities. For instance, you are at a public meeting. The discussion is about closing the state mental hospital. You are free to speak for or against, but you have a responsibility before you speak to know what you are talking about. You must have researched your subject."

A lively discussion followed, but most nurses agreed this was a new concept and very important. The next lecture would still be concerned with other responsibilities. Strange how much we take for granted.

R.R.#1 Halfmoon Bay B.C.
March 3/59

Dear Mary,

George and the children have just left for school so I decided to write to you while I have my last cup of coffee before I start to work. We are all fine here except George & he has a terrific cold. I hope it won't be as bad as mine was.

It is a beautiful morning. There is a low mist over the lake but the sky is blue and it looks just beautiful over the lake. David went out fishing this morning after breakfast but didn't get anything. The boys are having a wonderful time fishing these days. They have lots of action even though they don't land all their fish.

We were very sorry to hear about Larry. When we first heard it over the radio, we were positive Jim was on the plane because when they were here last Friday Jim said he was going back on Monday. We had some anxious hours before they identified the fifth body.

George went to see the Laskso's & the place was sold. There is still a remote possibility that you can still get it. The deal isn't completely wound up yet so time will tell.

2

George was going to write you a nice long letter but he is feeling so miserable that I know he won't feel like it. However he will as soon as he feels a little better. He writes a much more interesting letter than I do. I am a very poor letter writer & admit it.

Mr & Mrs. Haskins will be back to-day & so I must go & check their place over & make sure I have left nothing undone. It will be nice to have them back again even though they try us dreadfully, It's kind of nice to have them around.

We have the childrens room on the new house about ready for painting now. Its going to be a lovely room. Its not really as large as I would like but large enough. Its going to be the choice room in the house. It looks out at the creek at the back & when we get it all landscaped it will be really beautiful.

Kathy is very proud of it & tells me she thinks its the nicest room in the house. With the new room added on, our little house looks quite spacious & imposing. I can't believe we have built it ourselves.

3

You will be please to hear this, I think Kathy is completely over her infatuation with Holly. They are still friends but Kathy doesn't bother with her the way she did before. She is going with Shirley Goldrup & Maureen Donnely now. They are more her own age too.

It makes a great difference in Kathy. Holly is much too old for her & I think she knows it now. As soon as the weather warms up Kathy wants some of the girls to come out for the weekend & they will have a pyjama party in one of the cabins. She is constantly asking me when she can go swimming so I tell her "anytime, now if she wants" but she won't go.

This week is Education week & they are having a parents day at the school. Gary's class is having a puppet show I think. I am not an expert at making puppets but he is very proud of it.

David has started playing basketball & he tells us if he works very hard he may get to play in the Junior tournament so I think he is spending all his free time at school practicing.

Don't you think Gary has improved tremendously in his spelling?

4

They all seem to be doing well in school. I hope their next report cards show it. They all come home at nights now to tell us they got 'A' in their work.

We're enclosing some school pictures. Poor Kathy is very ashamed of her picture but I think its kind of cute. Gary's & David's are quite good though.

Well, it broad daylight now & high time I was getting to work so will close for this time. I'm so glad you are enjoying your work & are getting used to the weather there.

Love from all of us
Wynne.

Halfmoon Bay B.C.
March. 1, 1959

Dear mom—,

How are you? We are all fine. Glad
to hear your throat and coughs
etc. There was a fishing derby here.
Jack Goldrup and 4 other men.
The prize was a case of bear. Gary
entered it. He came second. Gary
and I ride in the back of the truck
now its lots of fun. Gary's fish
weighed 2 lbs 2 oz. Larry Lytell,
Bert, his son and son inlaw. Were
flying to Redonda Bay. I'll not

2

waste words were killed. There was an
unidentified person for two days.
We thought It was Jim for sure but
it turned out to be someone from
Campbell River excuse spelling.
Surprising or not though I got ""A"""
in Spelling & Reading. We had 2
fried chicken today for supper we
also had potatoe salad. I baked
tarts today apple tarts. 16 of them.
I have bought some material for
making myself a skirt. It is a
pretty color.

3

I won't start making it till tomorrow. When we got the sewing machine over I got a new blue sweater. The house is coming along fine. We are finished our room except for the painting and tiling. I went to the basket ball game friday. There are two skunks living under the house. We had to poison them much to our sorrow. I liked the Negro book. Gary got a haircut. We have a new boy in our room. He's sure a creep.

4

Stupid too. Our school pictures arrived. Mine turned out horibble. Gary's is good. We went to Garden Bay yesterday. I saw Carol and Dode and Holly. Gary's class had a red cross sale. Aunt Wynne baked for it.

Yours affectionatly
Kathy White

X O X O X O X O X O X O X O
X O X O X O X O X O X O X O
Lots of love

swalk
swalk

R.R. 1 Halfmoon bay
Sunday March 1.

Dear Mom

I have coagt 2 fish one 10 onces
and one 2 pounds 2ounces. I
enterd a fishing derbey and lost
by an inch. My fish was 2 pounds
2 ounces.

I cought my 2 fish with Uncle Goreges
fly rod. The prize was a case of
beer. Larry crashed his plan when
he was taking loggers to Rdonda
bay. He was five miles from his
logging camp. He sarted a Comox.
They thought there was 4 men abord
but ther was a unidentifid berson
absard from Camble rivr. We
thought it was Jim but it wasn't.
I got a new corduroy shirt. We went
to a backet ball game. We think
we have to poisend 2 skunkes one
feefal and one maile.

Aunt Win cut my hair. We had
chiken for supper. I have grown
quit a bit since I came hear. I
stayed at Michel Saterday.

Your Son Gary

OOOOOOOOOOOOOOOOOOOOOOOOO
XXXXXXXXXXXXXXXXXXXXXXXXX

Chapter 10

๑฿๑

WHEN ROSE ARRIVED IN CHICAGO in January of 1959. Presbyterian St. Luke's Hospitals had just merged into a thousand patient complex funded with private funds mostly from the Episcopalian Church (Anglican Church in Canada) and Presbyterian. There were many distinguished doctors who were paid salaries.

1948 was the first underwriting by the Federal Government of nursing education and the first time nursing classes were offered at Presbyterian on a racially and religiously non-discriminatory basis.

In 1941 the Chicago Medical Centre District was created by the state legislature and given power to buy and clear slum land. Presbyterian and the University of Illinois were in the district. So were Cook County Hospital and its affiliate, the Loyola University.

Prior to 1954 private patients were not used for teaching purposes and were separated from non-paying poor people. After this, thanks to Dr. Campbell, all patients became teaching patients and could be roomed together. The paying patients appreciated the extra attention they received.

When the merger of the two hospitals took place top nurses were in charge of all nursing activities. Barbara Schmidt and Dorothy Jane Heidenreich developed policy and a new type of procedure manual mentioned here because Rose had the opportunity to study the manual. She liked the simplified one page directions and brought the ideas back to Canada, to St. Mary's Hospital in New Westminster. Many nursing text books were written by nursing instructors at Pres. - St. Luke's and used across U.S.A. and Canada. Rose was delighted to be a small part of this beautiful hospital complex.

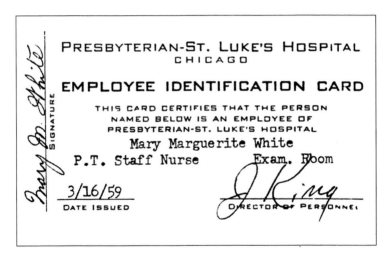

PRESBYTERIAN-ST. LUKE'S HOSPITAL
CHICAGO

EMPLOYEE IDENTIFICATION CARD

THIS CARD CERTIFIES THAT THE PERSON
NAMED BELOW IS AN EMPLOYEE OF
PRESBYTERIAN-ST. LUKE'S HOSPITAL

Mary Marguerite White
P.T. Staff Nurse   Exam. Room

3/16/59
DATE ISSUED   DIRECTOR OF PERSONNEL

"Why don't you apply to Pres. St. Luke's Rose. You could work there on your day off. We all work like that when we need extra money for family or holidays."

"If only I could, that would surely help. That is unheard of where I come from. No one works in two hospitals at the same time. Thanks for suggesting it. I will go tomorrow on my day off."

The interview went well. Rose was asked to report for orientation the next day. She was thrilled. This was a beautiful private hospital with one of the most up to date nursing departments in the country.

That evening Rose attended another lecture at Loyola. One of her classmates, who worked as an industrial nurse, had trained at the Vancouver General Hospital. She and Rose became friends. Her uncle, Dr. Brock Chisholm, a doctor from Vancouver General Hospital, had been head of the World Health Organization. Kay explained to Rose that about forty-five or more years ago he had warned that organization that something must be done to stem the overpopulation of the world or there would be a disaster, but little, if anything has been done to this day.

At that point the instructor came into the room.

"We'll continue our lecture on democracy with more areas of responsibility. We've said that if you are going to contribute to a public forum you have a responsibility to know the subject. For example, if you are not an engineer you would not state how a bridge should be built; if not an architect, how a building should be constructed. I think you now all understand this concept."

"You are all health professionals. This is your expertise, but did you know each citizen in a democracy has the responsibility to take care of his or her health? Which means, as you know, doing everything in moderation - eating, drinking alcohol, smoking, exercising, etc."

"Each of us has a responsibility to earn a living and to pay taxes. Each has a responsibility to get the best education available and to continue their education throughout their lifetime."

"Pericles said long ago, 'We do not say that a man who takes no interest in politics is a man who minds his own business; we say that he has no business here at all.' Each of us has a responsibility to help their country by running for public office when needed in their communities. In a democracy citizens are required to show selflessness, courage, teamwork and a sense of the common good. Each has a responsibility to do volunteer work when and where it is needed."

"Freedom - yes, you have freedom. But freedom has a price. You must make it work by being the best and doing your best at all times."

Again a heated discussion followed as these nurses were all leaders in their profession.

"Yes, Kay?" the instructor nodded.

"It sounds as if you are saying that in a democracy we are responsible for our own lives as opposed to a socialist government who takes that responsibility from the citizens. Is that what you mean?"

"You will study these thoughts I am sure." the teacher smiled.

Rose went back to the nurses' residence hoping for letters from her children. She was disappointed. The next day she went downtown on the city bus to shop for clothes and easter gifts for the kids. This was entertaining as the Americans have a different style. She was able to find jackets for the boys and a dress and shoes for Kathleen. However, she was shocked when she came out of one shop to find herself in a fierce electrical storm with the boldest lightning and the most frightening thunder she had ever heard. She cowered in a doorway out of the belting rain until she was able to catch a bus home.

The house the children talk about.

Taking the children to vancouver.
The new jackets.
Poncho.

R.R.1
Halfmoon Bay
March 15, 59

Dear Mom;

The reason this letter will be messy is because I burned all the fingers on my right hand except my baby & thumb finger. It all happened when I was sitting around the stove on a stool. I was reading the library catalogue. And the stool tipped somehow or other. To stop falling I put my hand on the stove and burned it. We went to the show called the yearling on Saturday. You may think it's about a horse but its not. Its about a boy and his fawn it was a really good show. Gary provided our supper on Saturday. It was fish. I baked some cup cakes a few burned though. Aunt Wynne has to layed the tiling in our bedroom and the bathroom. She is starting to tile her & Uncle Georges room. Uncle George built the clothes —

2

closet a few days ago. He is working hard at the cupboards in the kitchen and bathroom. Its really coming along. Uncle Goerge had a stiff neck but it feeling better now. Glad to hear your throat is feeling better. I got a new horse in Sechedt Wendnesday. I didn't go too school because of my finger. He's a pretty horse, I also gots some jacks. Thanks for shoes and dress. Has not arived yet though. I'M interested in how much a pair of shoes is that are on sale 4 for $1.00.

Hope I"m not being nosey in asking if so don't tell me for I'm sure they aren't $.25 a pair. How are you? I'm fine we all are. Goodbye for now lots of love.

> Your loving
> daughter
> Kathleen

XXOO
OOXX

P.S. Aunt Wynn is a bit cranky today very.

1

R.R.1 Halfmoon bay B.C.
Mar. 15. 1959

Dear Mom,

I suppliyed our supper Saterday.
I think I so a turtle tonight. I
forget ware I left of in the Gippsy
Colt would you please tell me in
the next letter. We have went to an
other show since. It was about the
Yearling. It was about a boy and a
dear. At fearst the boy was laying
by a pond for so alon win dear
apear out of the brush, then a
mother and 3 baby racksons came
to the stream. The boys dad was a
wounderful man. Ther was a bear
that they could She foot the were
going aftr she foot thrught brush,
water forrest when they meat up
with the bear the man said boy
you had better stay hear, but the
boy said no I an't scard when the
man was

2

to fiyer the gun the boy was halfway
up a tree Continued. The teacher
said I look just like the boy in the
picture exept that I do not waer
buck skin cloths. I will not forget

waer I am becaise I wright down the last sentens in a pad. The day befor yesterday the skunk was out on the forranda eatting the cats food So I skard him away then went outside and sat on a stump. And wated for him to come out. Finly he came out. He came running along over to the cats food. They are quit tame now.

Your Son Gary

X X X   O O O
X X X X X X   X   O O
X X X X X X   X   O O

R.R.I. Halfmoon bay B.C.
March 26, 1959

Dear Mom

I caought 2 fish and gave them to Mrs. and Mr. Haskins, the had them for supper. If I didn't get them they woudn't had supper. We have moved into our new house. Owers room is yellow and green. Kathy has my old bed and David and I are sleeping in his old bed. We have green tiling in ouer room. They have mottel colord tiel. We have got the lighting plant hooked up and now have Electric light. It has been raning since we got out of school. Uncle Goreges Aunt is coming to stay for a week. Uncl Gaeg and Aunt Win went to the stor this moring. Twinker fell in the water. Where having hotcross buns and eggs for breakfast. It has started to ran again.

How are you I am fine. Shanans came up this week. I only saw them once. Thank you for the easter things, we made prity Easter eggs.

(GARY)

Gary at Pender Harbour.
Second prize.

Chapter 11

❧

Chicago, March 1959

Dear family, Wynne and George,

I have been very sad since receiving your letters about the men killed in the plane accident. Jim also wrote and I know how upset he is. It is too bad not to get the lot near the lake. You have all made it sound so beautiful, especially when I compare it to the life here in Chicago. Life is strange. Maybe there is a special reason we missed this purchase. Only time will tell.

Gary, what a thrill to come second with your fish! I am quite glad a nine year old boy did not win a case of beer. I am sorry, too, that you had to kill the skunks. I guess you remember the weasel and the skunk under our cabin in Lac Le Jeune? We had to move out the next morning and lucky we didn't suffocate during the night after the weasel attacked and the skunk sprayed up through the cracks in the floor boards. Gary, I am sure it is Aunt Wynn's good cooking that makes you grow like that.

Wynne, I feel that you and George are really enjoying the children. I am happy for you. Their letters are such a joy. I shall be sad to take them away from all the nice things you are doing for them, giving them a taste of a real home. They sound so happy and interested in all they are doing. I will never be able to thank you nor will I be able to duplicate their experience but only give them once more a single parent.

I am sorry about the loss of the property. Guess it wasn't meant to be. What a shock about Larry and the others. Jim is very upset. He and Larry were very close friends. Thank you all for writing to me. I love you so much.

Hello David. When you get my next letter I will be working at Presbyterian St. Luke's Hospital on my days off from Cook County. I am glad you are getting a chance to play basketball and that you are doing better at school. This will make your life more fun.

Hello Kathleen. I hope your hand is healed up by now. It must have been quite painful. You were brave to cook muffins so soon afterwards. The house sounds lovely. Glad you are getting a chance to help decorate and make it into a home.

Love to everyone.

Mom.

XXX XXX XXX OOO OOO OOO

Chapter 12

THE DEVIL HIMSELF MUST HAVE gotten into Rose this day. She had always been intrigued that the administrator was called "The Warden". She saw a blonde young resident doctor coming towards her.

"The Warden wants to see you in his office," she said. The poor chap turned shades whiter and disappeared up the staircase.

"Now, why did I do such a mean thing? The warden will be equally surprised!" Rose thought.

She was wondering about something else. Mayor Daly had quite a reputation among the nursing staff who felt that there was corruption which passed down the chain of civic employees, including staff at Cook County. Certainly, there was little money available for such necessities as face cloths, towels and bedding. Rose had never seen a whole face cloth or towel, only what she classed as rags. The kitchen equipment was very old, just a rusty two burner gas plate to heat the food. These rose could accept without comment. However, something else was troubling her. The children, well under sixteen years of age, would be given a pre-operative sedative of one and a half grains of a barbiturate, enough to put an adult to sleep for hours, but it seemed to have no effect on these kids. Quite often the dose would be repeated and still the child would go to the operating room awake. It was some time before she figured out the barbiturate had been removed from the capsule somewhere down the chain and sugar, or whatever, substituted. She resolved, at some risk, to report her suspicions, but she would do it carefully.

It was time to report to Pres - St. Luke's for orientation. The contrast was unbelievable as it should have been. This was a new, privately endowed, hospital complex. Her most vivid memory was the psychiatric wing on the seventh floor. The single rooms resembled luxurious hotel rooms with day beds made up with attractive linens.

In one empty room, the nursing instructor said, "When we first opened this unit we put a patient in here and locked the door. He disappeared. There was no way he could get out except to fall seven floors down and obviously he had not done that. He was missing for forty-eight hours before a staff member saw a tile in the ceiling move, and, of course, that is where he was.

The dining area for the patients ran along a wall of windows overlooking a court below. There were small attractive tables seating four, with plants around that you would find in any first class restaurant. It was, indeed, a pleasant surprise.

With her orientation completed, Rose was assigned to the emergency area which, she thanked God, was nothing like Cook County.

R.R.1. Halfmoon Bay, B.C.
Wed April 1st, 1959.

Dear Mom,

How are you? You seem to be fine. I am fine. We have moved in the New House. Aunt Wynne baked bread yesterday. We just finished The house yesterday. Mom, do you room with another person too. What is her name. Hope you like the birthday present. We thought you might. To tell the truth I don't know what half of the tools are for but oh well. Shannons were up on the Easter weekend. So were Vicerstaffs. Smiths and Uncle Goerge's Aunt. They are all nice people to know. Vickerstafs have a girl 13 years of age. The dress was bit long but we just hemmed it so it looks very nice. But I like the shoes best of all. Really. Though I think the socks are nice too The hair ribbon is very pretty.

Turn over

Coulor Schemes

We are not sure but we think 3 living-room walls will be a light grey | green Our room is a nice yellow shade with a blue sort of trim. The utility room is a bright yellow we think The adjoining kitchen and living room wall are gray. We are not sure of the bathroom coulor. We went over to Haskins to play Scrabble. The shoes fit fine I just love them. April fools the house is not finished.

Lots of Love
Kathy

X X O O
X X O O
X X O O
X X O O
X X O O
X X O O
X X O O
X X O O

P.S. Write soon
Am glad to hear from you.

R.R.1 Halfmoon Bay
British Columbia
April first

Dear Mom.,

How are you feeling. I'm sorry I haven't written to you for such a long time. My report card was much better this time. Lots of people were at the lake this weekend and I helped Uncle George by taking care of them. Uncle George is now in town looking after the big bus, we expect him home tonight. Gary and I beat Kathy and Mrs. Haskins at a game of scrable. We had some decious fritters for supper tonight. Just remembered your birthday but I'm not sure wheather it was on Mar 26th or Mar 29th but anyways

There will be a birthday present with this letter. It will not be long before were togeather again. I hope we will be able to stay here for the summer holidays. We are now moved in the new house and is it ever pretty.

Your son David

R.R.I. Halfmoon Bay
April 7, 1959 Tuesday

Dear Mom;

The boys sure like their jackets the reason we didn't write sooner is we were moving in and were very busy. Granny Bower sent us some Easter candy which was very good. Mr. Itter, Carol Itter the swimming instructress before Janet. Its her father came up for about 4 to 5 days. We went to The show of 20,000 leagues under the sea again. It seemed more interesting this time though. Mr. Itters is a very interesting man very nice too. My garden is growing. Mrs. Old Haskins is sending me some sweet William to plant. The Boys jackets are very nice. Aunt Wynn and I saw the otter again today. It's sure cute, Only trouble is Smoky chased or barked at it. Mrs. Haskins sent over some oat cakes which are very good. Gary and I went swimming Monday. The water was cold but it was fun. Two of my girl friends are coming up at the same time 2 weeks from now you are a very good typewriter. I am practising to go in the variaty show on April 24, 1959, with 5 other girls. It is real fun. Wish you could see it.

Lovingly Kathy

XXXXXX
OOOOOO

turn over

P.S.
Hope you are well sorry to hear of
the bad storm.

R.R.I.Halfmoon Bay B.C.
April 7, 1959

Dear Mom

We have resevd the jackets and they
fite. I went over to Mrs. Haskins and
had tea. Aunt Win and Uncle Goreg
went to the store to. Some people
wore up looking at some properdey.
Uncle Goreg forgot about the mail
run and was late twice. Uncle Goreg
went to a meating tonight. Kathy
and I went swimming. We have
an ofel lot of coths so don't send
tomeny coths because we have lots.
My garden of bleading harts is in
blowm. Smoky is going nuts after
a fly. MR. Feldus walked down the
hill in Feb. Miss Haskins sent us
some cookies and we had them for
supper with ice cream. I have been
irited to go to Hodum — sound
with Michel. I cought a Butterfly
tonight.

Your Son Gary

X X X X X X X X X X X X X X X X X X X X X X X X X X X X X X X X X X
X X X X X X X X X X X X X X X X X X
O O O O O O O O O O O O O O O O O O O O O O O O O O O O O O O O O O O O
O O O O O O O O O O O O O
O X

April 8, 59

Dear Mom.

How are things in Chicago now.
Every thing is fine hear. We went
fishing tonight but didn't get a
bite. Uncle George is at a schoolboard
meeting at Gibsons. I made some
scores, passes and some kicks in a
game of football today. Gramma
Bower sent us a great box of nice
Easter candy for easter and so
did Auntie Wynne and Uncle George
give us some. Thank you for the
jacket all the kids wished they had
one. I don't need shoes because I
am well stalked I have two pairs
of runners and a good pair of
oxfords. I have rubber boots and
Uncle Jocks army boots. If you
want to get me some, my size is
81/2. I would like a nice pair of
charcoal pants though. I hope you
are feeling well.

Your Loving Son
Dave

P.S. Thank you for the stamps

Chapter 13

❧

Chicago, April 10, 1959

Dear Dave, Kathleen, Gary and Wynne and George,

Your letters are so interesting. All of you are improving your writing and spelling. Dave, I know you would help Uncle George. I believe you are enjoying Aunt Wynne's cooking. I could almost taste the fritters! Gary, you are certainly some good fisherman. The fish must taste so good when you just catch them, fry them and eat them. It is nice you are able to go to the movies, too, and the ones you have been to must remind you of Sakinaw Lake. Just imagine getting that close to skunks. They are beautiful, aren't they?

I am glad your new clothes fit. Granny Bower is the best mother and grandma that I know. Thank you for my birthday present. Just what I wanted!

Chicago is still exciting. The new hospital is very beautiful. The staff are really nice to me. I was afraid they wouldn't take me when my regular hospital couldn't tell me a week ahead when my days off would be, but they just said, "That's O.K., Mrs. White. You just come over on your days off and we will fit you in." I am learning a lot about how to treat staff with respect.

At Easter brunch in the hospital lunch room many of the staff brought their children from Sunday school. I had never seen so many healthy negro children, all dressed up in their very best clothes. The little girls were beautiful with ribbons in their hair, pretty ruffled dresses and patent slippers. You couldn't help but love them.

I am enjoying my school classes and learning a lot that I didn't know about democracy.

It won't be long until I am finished here, then you can show me all those things you have been telling me about. The new house sounds so inviting, and to think you all helped make it! I'm so proud of you all, including Wynne and George.

XXX XXX XXX	Love from	X X
OOO OOO OOO	Mom	O O

"To-night we are going to talk about leaders. There are basically three types: laissez-faire, dictator, and democratic. We will briefly discuss each type, then spend time on the democratic leaders'

qualities and goals which is what you are here to learn.

"Laissez-faire–leave it to him, lackadaisical, apathetic, indifferent, passionless, unresponsive."

This reminded Rose of a supervisor she once had. Rose was having difficulties on her nursing station and wanted the advice from this senior nurse. Her answer was, "And this too shall pass", and away she went.

"An autocratic leader, as you know, is a dictator. He or she is dogmatic, despotic, and arbitrary. They dominate, control and command. They keep mastery of the group and exercise absolute power. Our classic example is Hitler."

"A democratic leader is someone very different. Harry E. Fosdick said 'Democracy is based upon the conviction that there are extraordinary possibilities in ordinary people.' A democratic leader will search out these qualities in those who come under him and allow each person to spread their wings. He will show the way."

"You would be well advised to study the background of each staff member, their education, their interests, their experience, and then let them use this knowledge for the benefit of their area.

"When you take on a new leadership position I advise you not to be "the new broom that sweeps clean" but for some time to fit in and learn what is taking place before you change anything, otherwise you will find the old staff will sabotage your undertakings."

"The word 'democracy' comes from the Greek 'demos', people, 'krateein' to rule. It denotes political and social equality. It means justice for all.

"Perhaps I can give you another bit of advice. When you assign a task, check to see if it has been carried out as you directed and, if so, tell the member they have done as you wished, or give praise if deserved. If you do not follow up there is no incentive to do well."

Rose tried to remember when this had happened to her. She could not think of a single instance.

Again a lively discussion followed.

This particular night, Kay Cunningham had invited Rose to spend the night at her home in Oak Park, a beautiful residential area of Chicago. There was a full moon shining softly through great spreading trees and glimmering on a small lake surrounded by lush green lawns. It was the only time she was to see this area of Chicago, and she loved it.

It was during this visit that Kay told her about Dr. Brock Chisholm and dire predictions of the world population explosion.

"Kay, did I tell you the little story Wynne wrote about my youngest son, Gary who is staying with her and George? She saw him leave the house early Sunday morning with his B.B. Gun. About an hour later he returned with a grouse he had shot and plucked the feathers. After showing it to her at seven o'clock in the morning, he went into the bedroom where George was still sound asleep. He went over to the bed and plunked the plucked grouse on George's chest. George opened one eye to see one eye of the poor grouse looking back at him.

I almost feel reluctant to go back and take them away from the wonderful time they've had."

It was good to tell her thoughts to Kay. She was from the Vancouver area and knew how Rose was concerned about her little family.

At the end of the last class the group of nurses were reluctant to part without a little celebration. They decided to have dinner in a hotel near the Water Tower. They trooped through the door and made a lively group at a long table. Rose noticed many of the other diners staring at them. She thought this was unusual for they were only a rather ordinary group of women. However, when they got outside after the meal one of the American nurses heaved a great sigh of relief. "I was afraid they would refuse to let us in?"

Why?" Rose asked, truly puzzled.

"Because we had two negro nurses with us and negroes are not welcome in this dining room."

Dear Mom,

We are writing a five paragraph essay at school. I have done some fishing but haven't got much. Won't it be nice when you get back and its not to far away. Did you receive our present in the mail. We hope to be going to a show day after tomorrow. I have just finished reading quite a few books. I have been having a lot of fun at school now. The chicken coop will soon have its roof and floor. Gary is just going to have some Ice cream and I will soon join him. We are brewing some root beer which I hope turns out. Twinker had he kittens but only two and both were huge.

Dave White

Chapter 14

᭫᭪

Dear Mom;

How are you? I am fine. Hope you
are well. I'm having two girlfriends
up this weekend. They are real nice
kids. One of them is the girl I had
up last hallo'we'en. She is real nice.
Real glad to hear you're coming
home soon. I am in the variety
show on the 24th of this month.
Five othe girls are too. Its lots of
fun wish you were here to see me.
Twinker has had her kittens quite
a while ago. I thought you knew
though or I would have told you

117

sooner. She had them while we were at school. Uncle Goerge drowned them though. She had them a long time ago. Whats new with you? Have you any new clothes. Suppose you are busy writing exams. Can hardly wait till you get home. (Mr. Freeman) Mr.. Freeman asked the class to each write a Limerick and let the other teachers judge the best ones. He's giving a dollar to the winner. The first line has to be. with what I'm going to say.

If I had a jet propelled plane
I would soar down the airway lane
I'd take off at night
And scream with delight
As I flew from Vancouver to Blane

by
Your daughter
Miss Kathy White
Ha Ha

for the one I love

P.S. Turn Over

I heard Mrs. Sunkwist was sick and that her dog is stay with Wests.
We got our reports. I had a good one. I improved a lot. Did not go down in any thing have to write to Granny now bye.

R.R.1. Halfmoon Bay B.C.
Apr. Thursday 16, 1959

Dear Mom

I caught a trout as big as a sammon. They cut staks off of it. I didn't though because I was at Klines. When I was thar we went up the there loging camp — we saw seal lions black fish, porposes, blew sales and a eagle in its nest. Gordy shot a black bear but he didn't have enofe shells to kill it. Michel and I catherd 3 sack of ousters. We have cought lots of fish. I'm going swimming tomorrow. One of my freind won a 20 dollar bingo and my othere boyfreind won a 1 dollar bingo. I got a good repord her it is.

Language C
Spelling C
Reading C
Social Studies C
Health C
Physical Education C
Arithmetic U
Science C
Arts C
Music — C

Your
Son
Gary
XOXOXO

Dear Mom,

We have decided to right you 5 min
of a letter a day and send then
once a week. The house is coming
marvelously. The chicken coup
will be up this week. I changed the
course

2

of a creek and am now lanscaping
for a lawn. We are going to build
a water wheel and resevoir and
put trout in it. I haven't been out
fishing but I imagine it is getting
good, for two weeks ago a man
caught 6. Say hello to the kids from
me I got 80%

3

on my science test which was quite
high. I am starting to take more
interest in school now and hope
to improve my marks. Kathleen
is becoming quite a girl with a
needle and helps aunt wynne.
Aunt Wynne is not feeling to good
but is up on her feet. Gary is
now helping me with the wood on
back.

4

My name was in the paper for going to town. Uncle George is getting a bigger generator. One wall in our room in the new house is solid window. Aunt Wynne is getting ready for company for co. We hope that her two nephews are coming

All My Love
Dave W

XXXXXXOOO
XXXXXXXOOOOO
XXXOOO

R.R.#1 Halfmoon Bay B.C.
Thurs Apr 22/59

Dear Mary,

Just a note to add with the childrens letters to let you know alls well here. The weather has been just beautiful here - too good to last in fact. It was so hot out yesterday even David went swimming & he had swore he wouldn't go in till the middle of May.

It looks as if we are really going to get a public road down to the lake now. They (the public works) are just waiting for a bulldozer to come up from Gibsons & they will start. Its going to be very nice for us not to have to maintain the road ourselves any more & maybe our cars will last a little longer now.

The fishing has been very good this year, the best in years & the children have all been catching fish. In fact I am getting a little tired of fish. Gary spends most of his days out fishing. I've never seen a little boy who loves fishing so much as Gary does.

Kathy had a couple of friends up for the week end last week & they really had a lovely time. They stayed in a cabin & cooked all their own meals. The weather couldn't have been nicer for them either which was nice.

Kathy & Gary got their reports the other day.

2

They were both good. Kathy's was much better & Gary just fell down in Arithmetic. He is having a little trouble with his times tables but I think we can correct that soon. His spelling has improve so much that it really isn't a problem any more.

Our house is coming along slowly. There is still a tremendous amount to do & I sometimes wonder if we will ever finish - of course we won't - but it will be nice when we get it painted & the water working properly.

Well, its about time for George to be home so I must get this ready to mail & get ready to go & lay pipe so I'll say good-bye for this time & we will all write again in a few days. It is nice to think you will be back in a little over a month. The time has really gone fast hasn't it. When you get here I hope you will be able to stay & really have a nice long rest before you start off again.

Love from all of us.
Wynne & George.

R.R.I. Halfmoon Bay
April 24, 1959. Fri.

Dear Mom;

How are you? Hope you are fine. I am! Well tonight is the night I and six other girls in our class will be in the variaty show. We are in the Ball drill. When rehersing I think they all pretty well liked our act we got the biggest hand. Well its been rush rush rush all day today as soon as got home I had a bath and my hair washed and curled. I waiting for it to dry now. Gary passed his arithmetic test. His mark was 85% which is good. By the way these are all the tricks Poncho knows. Shake a paw, sit, jump through the hoop, roll over, dance and sometimes beg. I have just finished watering my garden. I have six pansie plants 2 of them give about four or 5 flowers each with a lot of buds. 2 others which are little ones you see they were not bought big they were tiny transplanters which are quite big. The first to Uncle Georges mother bought for me. They sure are pretty. Write soon.

Yours truly
Kathy.

P.S. Aunt Wynne has started to paint their room is it ever pretty.

Bye for now

X   X   X   O   O   O
O   O   O   X   X   X
X   X   X   O   O   O
OOOXXX

R.R.I. Halfmoon Bay B.C.

Dear Mom

I cann't catch fish any more I have tried everything I have and that isn't much. I can not use Aunt Wins and Uncle Goerges fishing takle and so I have only three spingers. We are going to hike up to Mount Arither and sleep ofer night. Also we are go to hike up to Killarny Lake. We are going to bouth Mount Arither and to Killarny with the cubs. The bus is at the boutom of the where working on a rode. I'm getting 85s and 86 in myarithmatic tests.

Dear Mom

I have caught two fish in the last two nights. I get 20% of all money taken from the boats which so far has earnned me $3.00. The chicken coup is now finished and I began wireing the grounds. We just paid a visit to Uncle Georges mother where we talked a lot. Gary is at cubs and aunt wyne and Uncle George have gone for him. The new house is almost completed, we just put the arborite on the counters. I haven't learned to drive yet but I am learning how it runs and the different parts. Your Loving Son Dave

R.R.#1 Halfmoon Bay BC
Mon May 5/59

Dear Mary,

The months are going by so fast I can't keep up with them. It doesn't seem possible that we are well into May already. And you will be back in about three weeks. We are all looking forward to seeing you & hope you will be able to stay & have a nice rest when you get here.

We got your letter today & you can rest assured that we will look after everything. There hasn't been anyone around & we will make sure that there won't be.

The children are all well & happy & looking forward to seeing you very much. The weather has been very poor lately so they haven't been doing any swimming but the boys have been doing a lot of fishing. Kathy has learned how to run the sewing machine & has hemmed quite a few of her dresses. Its amazing; when she came here all the dresses Carol Johnson gave her were much to big for her & now they just had to be taken up about two inches. I can't tell but I think they all have grown quite a bit.

We are getting more settled here all the time now. We have the cold water connected now & our next job will be to connect the hot water which shouldn't take too long then we will feel really

2

civilized. Of course there are still many things to do before the place will be finished but we can now take our time a little more then we did.

You will notice that Gary's letter has a sad note to it this time - I just found out to-night why. He had just lost my new flatfish when he was out fishing & hadn't told me about it. We had rigged up their rods & told them they couldn't use ours anymore & then he did & of course lost it. However now he has confessed & he is happy once more. I had noticed that he was wading in the last few days but had been too busy to wonder why. Poor Gary he was very sad. I didn't even scold him when he told me. I felt so sorry for him.

Cubs are over for the season now & I am very glad. He had been going over to Garden Bay on Tuesday & having dinner at Lyons & then going to Cubs with them and lately he has been getting fed up with Lyons. They & Gladys Klein are having a feud & Gary is sort of mixed up in it so all in all I'm glad its all over with. I didn't want to get mixed up in any feuds.

Well, my dear, its late & I have lunches to make yet so I will close for this time. Don't work too hard it isn't worth it you know & we'll be seeing you soon.

Love,
Wynne & George

P.S. Kathy is a candidate for May Queen & David is so proud he is nearly bursting.

Dear Mom

It sure won't be long before your home. We have almost got the water hooked up at the new house. Fishing has been very good and I am making more money than I can spend by taking care of the boats. For this I get 20% of the money. I have been working for a Mr. Smith and have quite a bit more to do for him. Did you know that Mr. & Mrs. Baker are divorced! I went to a bingo the other night & both Gary and I won. There are lots of deer on the highway now. I went to garden bay yesterday and had lots of fun. I got a raise in my allowance although I don't do much to earn it. It is almost dark and Gary is still fishing of the dock. Kathleen & Aunt Wynne & Uncle George are all reading. It has rained all ut today was nice. We just finished a good game of tag where we tried not to fight. Most of the house is painted now, only the fireplace to finish soon. Aunt Wynne and Uncle George a having a housewarming party and a party in a party to a Mr. Fletcher who did much to getting are new road. How is Jim, how did he take the news about Larry, Is he back

at his own camp. This is all I have
to say now.

Your Son
David

R.R.1. Halfmoon Bay B.C.
May 2, 1959 Sat.

Dear Mom;

I haven't heard from you for a long time what is wrong? Are you busy writing exams. We have painted the living – room light green and gray. The bedroom is dark green and pink. You know the colour of our room I presume. Quite a few people have been up renting boats lately. All the dogwood are out now and quite pretty. My garden is quite nice now. I have six pansies – all pretty. Afully glad to hear you're coming home. Will seem so nice. How're things going. Hope well. MR. Smith gave Aunt Wynne two planters today. We have the arborite glued down. I have my horses on the shelves in the bar. They are working the road now. The government should have it down soon.

We are picking the candidate for May Queen Monday.

Your daughter,
Kathy.

P.S.
Write Soon
Love
hugs

kisses

Am candidate
We have picked
them. Don't know
who is May
Queen yet though.

XOXO
XOXO

STUDENT'S NUMBER	STUDENT'S NAME	SCHOOL	SEM.	YEAR
6987 8	WHITE MARY M.	08	2	58 — 59

	CURRENT SEMESTER			CUMULATIVE TO DATE				
TRANS. HOURS	HRS. PASSED	HRS. ATT.	GRADE PTS.	AVERAGE	MISC. HRS	CREDIT HOURS		HRS. ATT.	LOYOLA POINTS	LOYOLA AVERAGE	MISC. HRS.
	3.0	3.0	0.90	3.0 0		TOTAL 0 0 3.0	LOYOLA PASSED 0 0 3.0	LOYOLA 0 0 3.0	0 0 9.0	3.0 0	

DEPT.	COURSE NO.	COURSE DESCRIPTION	GRADE	HRS. CREDIT	POINTS
NUED	251	PRINC OF SUPVS IN NU	B	3.0	9.0

WHITE MARY M
1900 W POLK ST
CHICAGO 12 ILL

LOYOLA UNIVERSITY
CHICAGO, ILLINOIS

MISC. HRS. FOR COM. STUDENTS ONLY

STUDENT GRADE REPORT
STUDENT

Chapter 15

ONE MORE SHIFT TO FINISH in County Hospital. As Rose looked back on a wonderfully productive learning experience she remembered, still with a thrill of appreciation, the head nurse yelling at the doctor, "You can go to Hell!" She remembered the times she had taken the little ones from their cribs to the door of the closed unit and allowed their negro mothers to hold their sick children. At that time this was not allowed. Because she was a mother Rose understood the need of this touch for both mother and child. The mothers were so grateful.

There was some unfinished business she did not look forward to but could not leave County until it was done. Rose reported her feelings that the barbiturate capsules given to the children had been tampered with and that someone was substituting the contents. The supervisor, a man, took her seriously and promised to investigate.

Chicago, May 15, 1959

Dear Family and Wynne and George,

This will be my last letter until we see each other. Sorry I haven't written. It's just that I've been getting ready to leave and, of course, doing some shopping for everyone.

This will be short. I enjoyed your letters and am looking forward to seeing all the things you have told me about, and I hope to eat some fish caught in your lake. Your school reports pleased me as did the improvement in your writing and spelling. Take care. I love you.

Wynne, I'll phone as soon as I arrive in Vancouver. Auntie Mayo, Uncle Jock and Jim will meet the train. All for now.

With hugs and kisses.

Mom

XXX   XXX   XXX   X X
OOO   OOO   OOO   O O

Rose packed her belongings, then reported to the Pres.-St. Luke's for one final afternoon shift. It was an unusually busy evening. Every cubicle was full as she and the slight young Canadian doctor tried to keep up. Around ten o'clock about ten people came storming in the door. A big negro man headed the group. They seemed to be pulling a bedraggled white female who scarcely seemed able to walk. The doctor explained, "There is no room available. Go over to the County Hospital emergency across the street." Very angry, the negro man shouted, "We'll go, but when she is settled I'm going to come back and get you and your nurse!" Rose believed him.

Next morning, with a tired sigh and a feeling of relief, she watched the Mississippi river fade behind her. Soon she would be at Sakinaw Lake where all that was dear to her resided.

Chapter 16

The Soul grows full by spending
The world's an empty cup
Until one's drinking from it
Fills it up.

Elsie A. McDowell
Beaver Mines, Alberta, 1935

THE TRAIN SEEMED TO CRAWL the last few miles, then suddenly they were in the Vancouver station. Waiting with happy smiles and tears were her friends since childhood, Auntie Mayo and Uncle Jock and her friend Jim from Pender Harbour. Tomorrow she would see the children.

What a welcome! Even if it was drizzling rain, there were all those happy faces, hugs and kisses galore. Wynne could hardly wait to tell Rose she was pregnant. She had been so busy she really couldn't say when it had happened. She was radiant and George was equally happy. (Note: the baby came a bit early but he came and stayed and has a brother two years younger, so "the old wives tale" came true for them).

It was a happy time. Everyone wanted to show off their efforts of all that passed while they had been apart.

Gary could hardly wait. "Mom, come out on the lake with me." Rose could see that fine Scottish mist, in fact a downright drizzle! She smiled and put on some warm clothing. Soon they were paddling away from the shore. A loon followed the boat closely. He called his haunting, eerie notes. Gary answered him. Back and forth they talked. "Mom, he always follows me."

Rose listened, deeply moved as she thought of the many hours the little boy, in her absence, had paddled the lake fishing and talking to the loon.

David

Gary

Kathleen

Harold & Betty Itter
Gary, Susan and Kathleen
David in back

ISBN 141206773-1

9 781412 067737